Intermediate
Data Analytic Skills

Databases, Programming, and Advanced
Statistics

Dr. Alex Harper

Table of Contents

Chapter 1: The Foundation of Intermediate Data Analytics

Why Intermediate Data Analytics Skills Matter

In the digital age, data is often referred to as the "new oil." But like oil, data in its raw form is not inherently valuable. It must be refined, processed, and analyzed to unlock insights that can drive better decisions. Intermediate data analytics skills bridge the gap between simple data observation and in-depth data-driven decision-making, equipping analysts to extract actionable insights from complex datasets. Let's explore how intermediate data analytics is transforming decision-making across some of the world's largest and most influential industries: healthcare, finance, and marketing.

1. Healthcare: Data Analytics for Precision Medicine and Operational Efficiency

Healthcare organizations generate enormous volumes of data every day, from patient records to clinical trial data and insurance claims. With intermediate data analytics skills, analysts can process this data to find trends that save lives, reduce costs, and improve patient outcomes.

Predictive Diagnostics: Intermediate analytics can help predict the likelihood of a disease by analyzing historical patient data and recognizing early signs of conditions. For instance, using regression analysis and machine learning algorithms, healthcare providers can identify patients at risk for chronic illnesses like diabetes or heart disease, enabling early intervention.

Optimizing Patient Care and Resource Allocation: By analyzing patterns in patient admissions and discharge data, hospitals can better allocate resources, predict peak times for specific departments, and streamline their staff scheduling to meet demand. Advanced data manipulation and statistical modeling help analysts interpret patient flow trends, ultimately improving efficiency and reducing waiting times.

Drug Development and Personalized Medicine: With vast amounts of genomic and clinical data, data analytics is helping to shape the field of precision medicine, tailoring treatments to individual patients. Clustering and classification techniques, applied at an intermediate level, are used to categorize patient data into meaningful groups, aiding in personalized treatment plans that align with each patient's unique medical profile.

2. Finance: Data Analytics for Risk Management and Fraud Detection

Finance is one of the most data-driven industries, where risk management, fraud prevention, and investment decision-making are heavily reliant on data insights. Intermediate data analytics plays a crucial role in ensuring the financial industry operates securely and profitably.

Risk Assessment and Management: Banks and financial institutions use intermediate-level analytics to evaluate the risk profiles of clients and potential investments. By employing logistic regression and other classification methods, analysts can assess which loans are likely to default or identify investments with a high risk of loss. This level of analytics provides insights that protect financial institutions from risky ventures.

Fraud Detection: Financial fraud detection is a priority across the industry, especially in the age of digital transactions. Data analysts use clustering and pattern recognition techniques to flag suspicious transactions, with advanced algorithms identifying anomalies that deviate from a customer's normal spending behavior. This proactive approach to fraud detection, which builds on foundational analytics, helps secure customer funds and maintain trust.

Portfolio Optimization and Market Analysis: Intermediate data analytics skills allow financial analysts to optimize investment portfolios by identifying trends and using predictive modeling. Time series analysis is particularly valuable for examining stock price trends and making informed predictions about market shifts. These insights support financial advisors and investors in making informed, data-backed decisions for wealth growth.

3. Marketing: Data Analytics for Customer Insights and Campaign Effectiveness

Marketing in the digital era is highly data-centric, with a focus on understanding customer behavior and optimizing campaign outcomes. Intermediate data analytics skills empower marketers to create targeted, impactful strategies based on deep insights.

Customer Segmentation and Personalization: Through clustering and advanced segmentation, marketers can divide their audience into distinct groups based on shared behaviors, demographics, or purchasing patterns. This enables personalized marketing that resonates more deeply with customers, increasing engagement and conversion rates. Intermediate skills allow analysts to run complex segmentation algorithms and identify meaningful patterns in large datasets, such as transaction history or website interaction data.

Campaign Performance Tracking and Optimization: Measuring the effectiveness of marketing campaigns is essential for budget allocation and strategy refinement. By applying intermediate-level statistical tests (e.g., A/B testing) and time series analysis, marketers can identify which aspects of a campaign are driving results and optimize their strategies accordingly. With these insights, companies can continually refine campaigns for maximum ROI.

Sentiment Analysis and Brand Reputation Management: In today's online landscape, customers often express their opinions about brands on social media and review platforms. Intermediate analytics enables sentiment analysis, a technique that uses text analysis and machine learning algorithms to gauge the public's perception of a brand. By identifying positive, negative, or neutral sentiment patterns, marketers can quickly adapt their strategies to protect or improve brand reputation.

Skill Advancement Pathway: How Databases, Programming, and Advanced Statistics Work Together

The journey from basic to intermediate data analytics involves mastering a set of complementary skills that transform data from mere numbers into meaningful insights. While beginner-level analytics often focuses on descriptive statistics and simple spreadsheet tools, intermediate analytics requires a deeper understanding of data management, programming for data manipulation, and statistical techniques for analyzing and interpreting complex datasets. By developing intermediate skills in databases, programming, and advanced statistics, analysts can bridge the gap between raw data and actionable insights, allowing for more impactful, real-world decision-making.

1. Databases: Efficiently Storing, Organizing, and Retrieving Data

Databases are essential for handling large volumes of data. As analysts move beyond basic analytics, they need to interact with databases to access and manage datasets too large or complex for typical spreadsheet software.

- **Understanding and Utilizing Relational Databases:** At an intermediate level, analysts must go beyond importing files and instead work with relational databases like SQL to store, retrieve, and organize data. Relational databases store information in structured tables, allowing for organized and efficient access to datasets through queries. Intermediate skills in SQL (Structured Query Language) enable analysts to perform complex data retrieval operations, such as joining tables and filtering datasets based on specific criteria.

- **Data Cleaning and Preprocessing in SQL:** Databases also support essential data-cleaning steps. Analysts learn to use SQL to preprocess data directly in the database by removing duplicates, handling missing values, and standardizing formats. This preprocessing stage ensures that data is ready for more advanced analysis, saving time and resources by minimizing the need for post-extraction cleaning.

- **Data Organization for Analysis:** With intermediate knowledge of databases, analysts can create views, indexes, and structured queries that organize data effectively. This preparation step is crucial, as it allows analysts to quickly access and pull data relevant to their analysis, making their work more efficient and reducing processing time.

2. Programming: Transforming and Manipulating Data

Programming skills, especially in languages like Python and R, allow analysts to go beyond what's possible in standard spreadsheet tools. Programming is key to handling large datasets, automating repetitive tasks, and performing complex data transformations.

- **Data Wrangling and Transformation with Python/R:** Intermediate programming skills enable analysts to use libraries such as Pandas in Python or dplyr in R to manipulate data. They can clean data by removing outliers, handling missing values, and performing transformations like normalizing and encoding categorical variables. This step is essential for preparing data for statistical analysis, making it more reliable and accurate.

- **Creating Reusable Code for Efficiency:** Programming also allows analysts to automate workflows by writing reusable code. For example, if an analyst is performing the same data cleaning steps for different datasets, they can create functions to apply these steps consistently, reducing the time and potential for error. Intermediate programming skills empower analysts to write these functions and scripts, streamlining their workflow and making complex analyses more manageable.

- **Combining Data from Multiple Sources:** Programming also enables analysts to integrate data from multiple sources, including databases, APIs, and flat files, into one cohesive dataset. This skill is especially valuable in intermediate analytics, where analysts often need to pull data from various sources, transform it, and merge it into a single file for analysis.

3. Advanced Statistics: Generating Deeper Insights from Data

Advanced statistical techniques allow analysts to move beyond descriptive analytics and make more sophisticated inferences and predictions based on the data. These skills are essential for tackling more complex questions, such as predicting future outcomes or identifying relationships within the data.

- **Regression and Predictive Modeling:** Intermediate statistics often begin with regression analysis, a powerful tool for understanding relationships between variables and predicting future outcomes. Linear and logistic regression are particularly useful for business contexts, where analysts can model relationships, like customer behavior or sales trends, and make predictions that inform decision-making. By mastering regression, analysts can add predictive power to their analyses, providing insights that go beyond what happened in the past.

- **Hypothesis Testing and Statistical Inference:** Intermediate analysts also learn to apply hypothesis testing and confidence intervals to test ideas and make data-driven conclusions. This skill is crucial for decision-making, as it allows analysts to validate assumptions and quantify the likelihood of observed effects. With these techniques, analysts can assess the significance of their findings, leading to more confident, data-supported recommendations.

- **Clustering and Segmentation:** Clustering methods, such as k-means and hierarchical clustering, are valuable for identifying patterns and segmenting data into meaningful groups. In marketing, for example, clustering can help identify customer segments based on purchasing behavior, which can then inform targeted marketing strategies. This type of advanced statistical analysis allows analysts to uncover patterns in the data that aren't immediately apparent, revealing insights that can guide strategic decisions.

Integrating Databases, Programming, and Statistics: A Cohesive Analytical Workflow

The real power of intermediate data analytics lies in the ability to combine these three skill sets into a cohesive analytical workflow. Here's how they come together:

1. **Data Retrieval and Preparation (Databases):** Analysts start by accessing and cleaning data from databases, ensuring that it's well-structured and ready for analysis.

2. **Data Transformation and Analysis (Programming):** Next, they use programming languages to transform and manipulate the data, creating new variables, standardizing values, and preparing datasets for analysis. This step also allows

them to automate repetitive tasks and work with data that may come from multiple sources.

3. **Insight Generation (Advanced Statistics):** Finally, they apply statistical techniques to generate insights, such as predicting trends, testing hypotheses, or segmenting the data into meaningful groups. By using advanced statistical methods, analysts can move beyond surface-level insights to provide deeper, data-driven recommendations.

In combining these skills, analysts transition from simple data observations to an in-depth analytical approach that adds substantial value to their organizations. Intermediate data analytics skills equip professionals to make informed decisions that drive positive business outcomes, proving the value of their analytical expertise.

Databases as the Heart of Data Storage and Retrieval

Understanding Relational Databases: The Backbone of Data Storage

In the world of data analytics, storing and managing data efficiently is fundamental to obtaining accurate, actionable insights. Relational databases, such as those managed with SQL (Structured Query Language), provide the structure and flexibility needed to handle large volumes of complex data. Unlike flat files or spreadsheets, relational databases organize data into related tables, allowing for streamlined data retrieval and ensuring consistency across datasets. Mastering relational databases is essential for intermediate-level data analysts, as it enables them to work with data in ways that are both scalable and efficient.

The Structure of Relational Databases: Tables, Rows, and Columns

At the core of relational databases is the concept of tables. A relational database organizes data into tables (also called relations), where each table represents a specific type of entity (such as customers, products, or transactions) and contains rows and columns.

- **Tables as Data Entities:** Each table in a relational database is structured to represent a single entity type, such as "Customers," "Orders," or "Products." By organizing data into tables, databases enable analysts to efficiently store and retrieve information without redundancy. For example, in a retail database, the "Customers" table might include columns for customer ID, name, and contact information, while an "Orders" table could track individual purchases.

- **Rows and Columns for Structured Data Storage:** Rows represent individual records within a table (e.g., a single customer or transaction), while columns represent the attributes or fields associated with each record (e.g., customer name, date of purchase). By defining clear columns for each attribute, relational databases ensure that data is consistently structured, reducing the chance of errors and making it easier to analyze.

- **Primary and Foreign Keys:** Relational databases use unique identifiers called primary keys to differentiate records within a table. In addition, foreign keys link related records across tables, forming relationships between them. For example, in a customer-order database, the "CustomerID" in the "Orders" table may serve as a foreign key that connects each order to a specific customer in the "Customers" table. These keys are essential for creating meaningful relationships between tables, allowing data to be connected and referenced efficiently.

The Importance of SQL in Data Management

SQL (Structured Query Language) is the standard language used for managing relational databases. SQL allows analysts to create, read, update, and delete data within a database, which is commonly referred to as CRUD operations. Intermediate SQL skills empower analysts to perform complex data retrievals, transformations, and analyses directly within the database environment.

- **Data Retrieval and Filtering:** One of SQL's most powerful features is its ability to retrieve data quickly and filter results based on specific criteria. Using SQL's SELECT statement, analysts can query specific columns and apply filters (using WHERE clauses) to retrieve only the data they need. For example, an analyst could use SQL to find all transactions over

$1,000 within a specific date range, providing valuable insights without needing to process entire tables.

- **Data Aggregation and Summarization:** SQL's aggregation functions (e.g., SUM, AVG, COUNT) enable analysts to perform calculations directly within the database. For example, by grouping transactions by customer ID and using SUM, an analyst can quickly calculate each customer's total spending. This ability to summarize data within the database is highly efficient, especially for large datasets, as it reduces the amount of data that needs to be transferred for further analysis.

- **Complex Joins for Multi-Table Analysis:** Relational databases excel at handling complex data relationships through joins, which allow data to be combined from multiple tables. SQL join operations (INNER JOIN, LEFT JOIN, RIGHT JOIN, FULL OUTER JOIN) enable analysts to pull related information across tables, making it possible to analyze interconnected datasets. For example, an INNER JOIN between the "Customers" and "Orders" tables allows analysts to connect each customer with their corresponding orders, providing a complete view of customer behavior.

Benefits of Relational Databases for Intermediate Data Analytics

Relational databases offer a structured, flexible, and scalable solution for managing data, making them invaluable for intermediate data analytics. Here's how they contribute to data analysis:

1. **Consistency and Data Integrity:** By organizing data into structured tables, relational databases ensure that data remains consistent across records. Relationships between tables are enforced through constraints (such as foreign keys), preventing issues like duplicate records or orphaned entries. This consistency is essential for data accuracy, as errors in data integrity can lead to flawed analyses and poor decision-making.

2. **Efficient Data Retrieval and Processing:** SQL allows analysts to query only the data they need, reducing processing time and minimizing memory

usage. For instance, rather than loading an entire dataset into a program like Python or R, analysts can use SQL to filter and retrieve only relevant data, making analysis faster and more manageable.

3. **Scalability for Large Datasets:** Relational databases are designed to handle large volumes of data. As companies generate more data, relational databases provide the scalability needed to store and retrieve information without compromising performance. This scalability is crucial for intermediate analysts, who often work with larger datasets that would be unwieldy in traditional spreadsheets.

4. **Security and Access Control:** Many relational databases offer built-in security features, allowing administrators to control access and permissions for different users. This is important for maintaining data privacy and security, especially when handling sensitive information, such as customer data or financial records. Intermediate analysts benefit from this control as it ensures that data remains secure while allowing authorized access for analysis.

Relational Databases in Practice: An Example

To illustrate the role of relational databases in data analysis, consider a company that uses a relational database to track sales, customers, and inventory. This company might have separate tables for "Customers," "Orders," "OrderDetails," and "Products."

- **Step 1: Organizing Data into Tables:** Each table is structured with relevant columns. The "Orders" table contains information on each purchase, while the "OrderDetails" table lists individual items for each order. This structure ensures that data is organized and accessible.
- **Step 2: Joining Tables for Analysis:** To analyze customer purchasing behavior, an analyst can use SQL to perform a join between the "Customers," "Orders," and "OrderDetails" tables. This join would connect each customer to their orders and items within each order, enabling a complete view of purchasing patterns.
- **Step 3: Applying Filters and Aggregations:** Using SQL's filtering and aggregation features, the

analyst can identify high-value customers, calculate total spending by customer, and determine the most popular products. By using SQL directly in the relational database, the analyst can obtain insights without needing to transfer large amounts of data to another tool.

Conclusion: The Role of Relational Databases in Intermediate Data Analytics

Relational databases are at the core of effective data storage and retrieval in intermediate data analytics. With a solid understanding of SQL and relational database structures, analysts can access, organize, and analyze complex data more efficiently, providing valuable insights that drive better business decisions. Mastering databases enables intermediate analysts to manage large datasets, work with interconnected data, and build a foundation for more advanced analytics skills.

Advanced SQL Queries for Intermediate Users

As you advance in data analytics, mastering SQL becomes essential, especially as your data grows larger and more complex. Advanced SQL skills enable you to move beyond simple SELECT queries and harness powerful techniques like joins, subqueries, and window functions. These features allow you to analyze relationships, retrieve insights from multiple tables, and work with grouped data in ways that transform raw data into actionable information. In this section, we'll explore some advanced SQL techniques, with practical examples and an explanation of how each is used in real-world data analysis.

Joins: Connecting Data Across Tables

In many databases, data is split across multiple tables. For example, a sales database might have one table for customer information and another for orders. To analyze a customer's purchasing behavior, you'll need to connect these tables to see which customers made which purchases. This is where joins come in.

There are several types of joins, but we'll focus on two common ones: INNER JOIN and LEFT JOIN.

INNER JOIN: Viewing Only Matching Records

Imagine you want to see only those customers who have placed an order. That's where an INNER JOIN comes in handy. By joining the "Customers" and "Orders" tables, SQL returns only the customers who have a corresponding order record in both tables. For example, when you join the two tables on the CustomerID, SQL connects matching records, allowing you to view customer names along with their order dates. INNER JOINs are especially helpful for cases where you only need data that exists in both tables, such as details of customers who actually made purchases.

LEFT JOIN: Including All Records from One Table

A LEFT JOIN, on the other hand, retrieves all records from the left table, regardless of whether there's a match in the right table. So, if you want a complete list of customers, including those who haven't made any purchases, LEFT JOIN is the tool you need. It pulls all customers into the results and fills in missing order details with NULL values for those who haven't placed any orders. This can be incredibly useful when identifying customers who haven't engaged recently, offering valuable insights for marketing campaigns.

Subqueries: Embedding Queries Within Queries

Subqueries, or "nested queries," are queries placed inside another SQL query. These are powerful tools for scenarios where you need to calculate something separately, then use it within a larger query. Subqueries let you handle complex data requirements in steps.

For example, imagine you want to identify customers who have spent more than the average amount. First, you calculate the average total spent, then pull only those customers who have spent more than this amount. In this case, a subquery calculates the average spending across all customers, while the outer query retrieves only those who exceed this average. Subqueries are particularly effective for comparisons, letting you retrieve values based on conditions you calculate on the fly.

Correlated Subqueries offer another layer of flexibility. Unlike standard subqueries, correlated subqueries reference columns from the outer query. They're useful when the inner query depends on values from the outer query to execute. For example, to find customers who have made an order over

$500, the subquery references the CustomerID from the outer "Customers" query, allowing it to match criteria across related tables seamlessly.

Window Functions: Analyzing Data Across Rows

Window functions are SQL tools that allow you to perform calculations across a set of rows related to the current row, known as the "window." They're especially useful for tasks like ranking, running totals, and calculating moving averages. Unlike aggregate functions that collapse rows, window functions retain all rows and simply add calculations alongside them.

For instance, **ROW_NUMBER()** lets you assign a sequence number to each row. Imagine you have a sales table and want to rank each sale based on the highest order total. ROW_NUMBER() helps by creating a sequence for each row, ranking sales from highest to lowest. This function is especially useful for ordered lists or leaderboards.

When you need to rank but want to handle ties, **RANK()** and **DENSE_RANK()** are helpful alternatives. They assign the same rank to tied values but differ in handling the sequence gaps created by ties. If two orders have the same total, both will receive the same rank, but the next rank will skip a number. These functions are essential when you want to maintain relative positions, even with duplicate values.

Finally, for cumulative calculations like running totals, **SUM() OVER()** is an invaluable tool. Let's say you want to calculate a running total of sales over time. SUM() OVER() allows you to do this directly within your query, tracking total sales progression row by row.

This query produces a cumulative total for each order, showing the ongoing sum of sales by date. Running totals are often used in financial and sales data to track growth over time, and window functions make it easy to calculate these within SQL.

Applying Advanced SQL Techniques in Real-World Analysis

Advanced SQL queries are foundational tools for intermediate analysts, offering the flexibility to connect data across tables, filter results based on complex conditions, and generate calculations that reveal deeper insights. Here's a quick summary of how these advanced SQL techniques can be used:

1. **Joins** let you combine tables, bringing together related information that's stored separately for efficiency and organization.

2. **Subqueries** allow you to create conditions and comparisons that use values generated within the query, ideal for layered data requirements.

3. **Window functions** enable powerful row-by-row calculations that preserve the data's structure, allowing for rankings, cumulative totals, and more detailed analyses.

By mastering these SQL techniques, you're equipping yourself with the tools to analyze complex data structures, make faster data-driven decisions, and add significant value to your data analytics projects. These advanced queries bring efficiency, depth, and flexibility to your analysis, helping you tackle real-world data challenges with confidence.

Programming for Data Manipulation and Analysis

Python and R in Data Analysis: Versatile Tools for Data Manipulation and Insights

As you transition to intermediate data analytics, programming skills become invaluable for handling complex datasets and performing advanced analyses. Two programming languages dominate the data analytics landscape: Python and R. Both are versatile, powerful, and widely used, but each has its unique strengths that make it suited to different types of data tasks. Understanding the roles of Python and R in data analysis will help you choose the right tool for the job and maximize your analytical capabilities.

Python: A Multi-Purpose Language for Data Manipulation, Automation, and Machine Learning

Python is a general-purpose programming language that has gained immense popularity in data science and analytics due to its flexibility, readability, and extensive library support. It's a go-to choice for many data analysts because it can handle everything from data manipulation and statistical analysis to automation and machine learning. Let's explore some key reasons Python is an essential tool for data analytics:

1. **Data Manipulation with Pandas and NumPy:** Python's Pandas and NumPy libraries are foundational tools for data manipulation. Pandas offers a DataFrame structure, similar to a spreadsheet, that allows analysts to load, manipulate, and clean data with ease. This includes handling missing values, filtering data, merging tables, and applying complex transformations. NumPy, on the other hand, is optimized for numerical calculations, providing the speed and efficiency needed for handling large datasets.

   o *Example:* If you have a dataset with missing values and need to fill those gaps based on specific criteria, Pandas allows you to quickly fill or replace values. For instance, you can use df.fillna() to replace missing data in a DataFrame.

2. **Automation and Workflow Efficiency:** Python's versatility allows you to automate repetitive tasks, streamlining your data workflow. By writing functions and scripts, analysts can automate data collection, data cleaning, and even report generation. This reduces manual effort and minimizes errors, especially when working with large, recurring datasets.

   o *Example:* You could write a Python script that connects to a database, extracts data, cleans it, performs analysis, and then exports the results, all in a single automated process. This is particularly useful for tasks that need to be repeated regularly, like weekly sales reporting.

3. **Machine Learning and Predictive Analytics:** Python is also highly regarded for machine learning due to libraries like Scikit-Learn, TensorFlow, and PyTorch. For intermediate-level analysts, Scikit-Learn offers accessible tools for building basic predictive models, such as regression and classification, without needing extensive knowledge of machine learning. These models can provide valuable insights into trends, forecasts, and customer behavior.

- *Example:* With Scikit-Learn, you can build a simple linear regression model to predict sales based on historical data, using only a few lines of code. Python's ecosystem allows you to quickly move from data manipulation to model building, all within the same environment.

4. **Visualization with Matplotlib and Seaborn:** Visualization is a critical component of data analysis, as it allows analysts to communicate findings effectively. Python's Matplotlib and Seaborn libraries offer a wide range of chart types, from basic line charts and bar plots to complex heatmaps and distribution plots, helping analysts to represent data visually.

  - *Example:* You might use Seaborn's sns.heatmap() to create a heatmap of correlation between variables, making it easier to spot relationships and patterns in your data.

In summary, Python is a powerful tool for data analysis because it combines flexibility, ease of use, and a comprehensive set of libraries. It's particularly useful for data manipulation, automation, machine learning, and visualization, making it a go-to language for analysts aiming to handle diverse tasks within one environment.

R: A Statistical Powerhouse for Data Analysis and Visualization

R is a language developed specifically for statistical analysis and data visualization, making it an excellent choice for analysts focused on data-driven insights, statistical modeling, and data exploration. While Python is more versatile across a range of applications, R excels in statistical analysis and is often preferred by statisticians and researchers. Here's how R supports intermediate-level data analysis:

1. **Data Wrangling with dplyr and tidyr:** R's dplyr and tidyr packages simplify data manipulation, allowing analysts to filter, arrange, group, and summarize data efficiently. Dplyr's syntax is straightforward and highly readable, using verbs like filter(), mutate(), and summarize() to make data transformations easy to understand and implement. Tidyr complements dplyr by helping to clean and

reshape data into a tidy format, essential for structured analysis.

- o *Example:* Using dplyr's group_by() and summarize() functions, you can quickly calculate average sales per region, making it easy to analyze grouped data.

2. **Advanced Statistical Analysis:** R was designed with statistics in mind, making it a natural choice for analysts focused on in-depth statistical modeling. Whether it's regression, hypothesis testing, or time series analysis, R has built-in functions and packages like stats, MASS, and forecast that make complex statistical tasks straightforward. R's statistical capabilities make it easier to perform advanced analyses, test hypotheses, and validate results with statistical rigor.

- o *Example:* R's lm() function allows you to run linear regression with just a line of code, making it quick and efficient for intermediate users to analyze relationships between variables.

3. **Data Visualization with ggplot2:** ggplot2 is one of the most powerful and flexible data visualization

packages available, allowing analysts to create high-quality, publication-ready visualizations. It's based on the grammar of graphics, which provides a structured approach to creating visualizations by layering components like axes, scales, and geometries.

- *Example:* With ggplot2, you can create complex visualizations like layered line charts and customized scatter plots. Using just a few lines of code, ggplot2 lets you produce visualizations that are both visually appealing and informative, enhancing your ability to communicate findings.

4. **Handling Big Data with R:** While R is often associated with smaller datasets, it has packages like data.table and specialized libraries (such as bigmemory) for handling larger datasets. These packages allow R to process larger data efficiently, although Python is typically faster for extremely large datasets. However, with data.table, you can work on larger datasets in R with greater efficiency, leveraging its advanced functionality for filtering and aggregating data.

5. **Interactive Data Exploration with Shiny:** Shiny is a unique feature of R that allows you to create interactive web applications and dashboards. This is particularly valuable for analysts who want to make their findings interactive and accessible to stakeholders. With Shiny, you can create web-based interfaces where users can explore data, adjust parameters, and view real-time results.

   o *Example:* You could create a Shiny dashboard that allows managers to explore sales data across different regions and time frames, providing a user-friendly interface that helps decision-makers interact with the data directly.

In summary, R is an exceptional tool for statistical analysis, advanced data visualization, and interactive data exploration. Its built-in statistical functions and visualization capabilities make it ideal for tasks that require deep statistical analysis and graphical representation.

Python vs. R: Choosing the Right Tool for the Job

When to use Python or R often depends on the specific requirements of your analysis:

- **Choose Python** when you need a versatile tool that supports a range of tasks, from data manipulation and automation to machine learning. Python's extensive libraries and flexible syntax make it ideal for analysts who want an all-in-one solution that scales from data preparation to model deployment.
- **Choose R** when your work involves in-depth statistical analysis, high-quality visualizations, or interactive data presentations. R's specialized statistical functions and visualization packages make it perfect for research-heavy environments and data-driven reporting.

For many intermediate analysts, learning both languages can be highly beneficial. While each has its strengths, Python and R can complement each other, allowing you to choose the best tool for each task and maximize your efficiency in data analytics.

By understanding the roles of Python and R, you can select the most effective tool for each analytical task, improving both the quality and speed of your data analysis. Both languages are invaluable assets, each offering unique features that enhance the way you handle, analyze, and visualize data. As you continue to develop your programming skills, you'll be equipped to tackle increasingly complex data challenges and provide deeper insights to your organization.

Key Libraries and Functions for Intermediate Data Manipulation

To perform data analysis effectively, it's essential to be familiar with specialized libraries that simplify data manipulation, transformation, and visualization. Python and R offer powerful libraries designed specifically for handling and analyzing data, each providing a wide array of functions that reduce the amount of code you need to write and increase the efficiency of your workflow. In this section, we'll explore some key intermediate libraries—Pandas and NumPy for Python, and dplyr and ggplot2 for R—and provide some power-user tips to make the most of these tools.

Python Libraries: Pandas and NumPy

Python's Pandas and NumPy libraries are foundational tools in data analytics, enabling intermediate analysts to manipulate and analyze data with precision and efficiency.

Pandas: The Data Manipulation Powerhouse

Pandas provides the DataFrame structure, a two-dimensional, table-like data structure that makes it easy to manipulate, clean, and analyze data. Here are some key functions and power-user tips for getting the most out of Pandas.

Filtering and Selecting Data with loc and iloc

To start, let's talk about two powerful methods in Pandas: loc and iloc. These methods help you quickly filter and select data from a DataFrame, which is essential for working with large datasets. loc is label-based, so you can use it to select rows and columns by their names, while iloc is position-based, helping you access data by its position in the DataFrame. This flexibility is valuable when you need specific rows or columns based on certain criteria. For example, if you want to select rows where a customer's age is over 30, you can use loc to do just that. It's a simple and efficient way to filter data based on conditions without needing complex syntax.

Chaining Methods for Cleaner Code

One of Pandas' strengths is the ability to chain methods together, letting you perform multiple actions in a single, streamlined line. This approach makes your code cleaner and more efficient, which is a huge help when working with data. For instance, instead of breaking up operations, you could filter, sort, and reset the index of a DataFrame all in one line. By chaining these operations, you keep your code concise and readable, which is especially useful for anyone maintaining or reading your code later.

Using GroupBy for Aggregated Analysis

The groupby function in Pandas is an incredibly powerful tool. It lets you group data by specific columns and perform aggregations like sum, mean, and count. This is particularly useful for summarizing data by category. Say you want to find the average purchase amount per customer; groupby makes this easy, providing insights into customer spending behavior by creating a summary of their average purchases.

Pivot Tables for Multi-Dimensional Analysis

Pivot tables in Pandas work similarly to those in Excel, giving you the ability to summarize data in a multi-dimensional format. They're perfect for creating cross-tabulations and quickly analyzing large datasets. Imagine you want to see the total sales for each product across different regions. A pivot table organizes this data in a clear, comparative format, making it easy to understand regional sales performance at a glance.

NumPy: High-Performance Numerical Computation

Now let's dive into NumPy, a library that complements Pandas with high-performance array operations, ideal for handling large-scale numerical data.

Creating and Manipulating Arrays

NumPy's array function creates arrays that are faster and more memory-efficient than Python lists. For example, creating a two-dimensional array gives you a compact, structured way to store and manipulate data, which is especially useful for large datasets.

Applying Vectorized Operations

One of the best features of NumPy is vectorization, which lets you perform operations on entire arrays without writing loops. For instance, if you need to multiply each element in an array by 2, you can simply multiply the entire array. This speeds up computation significantly, especially with larger datasets.

Statistical Analysis with NumPy

NumPy also provides a range of functions for statistical analysis, such as mean, median, standard deviation, and sum. These functions are perfect for quick, on-the-fly statistical summaries, saving you time and effort when you need to get a general sense of your data.

R Libraries: dplyr and ggplot2

R's dplyr and ggplot2 libraries offer a powerful toolkit for data manipulation and visualization, making them valuable for intermediate-level analytics work.

dplyr: Data Wrangling Made Simple

With dplyr, you have access to functions like filter, select, and arrange, which allow you to manipulate data in a readable, almost English-like syntax. For example, filtering rows where sales are above a certain threshold, or selecting only specific columns, becomes straightforward and intuitive.

Summarizing Data with Group By

Combining group_by and summarize lets you perform quick aggregations, which is great for calculating statistics across different categories. For instance, you can group your data by region and calculate average sales, giving you a summary of regional performance with just a few lines of code.

Transforming Data with Mutate

The mutate function allows you to create new columns or modify existing ones on the fly. This is perfect for adding calculated fields, like showing a 10% discount on prices, directly in your DataFrame. It's incredibly useful in financial and sales analysis, where creating derived metrics is a common requirement.

ggplot2: Advanced Data Visualization

The ggplot2 library, built on the grammar of graphics, is highly flexible and lets you create publication-quality visualizations. Starting with ggplot to define your data and aesthetics, you can then add layers like geom_point for scatter plots or geom_bar for bar charts, giving you control over your visualizations.

Faceting for Multi-Panel Plots

Faceting allows you to split your data into multiple panels, making it easy to compare subsets within the same chart. For example, creating separate plots for each region helps you visually compare trends across categories, which is incredibly useful for exploratory data analysis.

Customizing Visuals with Themes and Colors

With ggplot2, you have extensive customization options to make your visuals truly stand out. This includes applying themes, colors, and custom labels. By adding theme() and scale_* functions, you can adjust the look and feel of your charts to better fit your style or presentation needs. For example, using a minimal theme and adding color by region makes your charts cleaner and more visually appealing. It's a straightforward way to give your graphics a polished look while making the data easier to interpret.

Summary of Key Libraries and Power-User Tips

For intermediate data analysts, mastering libraries in both Python and R can significantly boost productivity and depth in analysis:

- **Python's Pandas and NumPy:** These libraries are ideal for data manipulation, numerical analysis, and data cleaning.
  - Use **method chaining** in Pandas for more concise and readable code.

- o Take advantage of **vectorized operations** in NumPy for quicker calculations across large datasets.
- **R's dplyr and ggplot2:** These are perfect for streamlined data wrangling and sophisticated visualizations.
  - o Apply **group_by** and **summarize** in dplyr for efficient aggregation and category-level insights.
  - o Use **ggplot2** to create layered, customizable charts that enhance the clarity and impact of your data storytelling.

With these tools, Python and R provide a powerful combination for efficient, insightful analysis and compelling visual communication.

By incorporating these libraries into your workflow, you'll streamline data analysis tasks, reduce code complexity, and create more effective visualizations. These libraries empower intermediate analysts to handle larger datasets and conduct more sophisticated analyses, adding significant value to their data analytics toolkit.

Hands-On Example: Extracting and Manipulating Data Using SQL and Python/R

In this hands-on exercise, you'll learn how to extract data from a SQL database and then manipulate it in Python or R. By combining these two powerful tools, you'll gain a deeper understanding of how databases and programming work together to create a seamless, efficient data analysis process.

Imagine you're an analyst at an e-commerce company. You want to analyze customer purchasing behavior to identify high-value customers and uncover trends in product purchases. The data you need is stored in a SQL database, but analyzing it directly in SQL is challenging. Instead, you'll pull the data into Python or R, clean and transform it, and generate insights that can drive marketing and sales decisions.

Step 1: Extract Data from SQL Database

First, we need to connect to the SQL database and extract the data. Let's assume you have two tables in your SQL database:

1. **Customers**: Contains customer information (CustomerID, Name, Email, Country)
2. **Orders**: Contains order details (OrderID, CustomerID, OrderDate, TotalAmount)

We want to retrieve customer information along with their total spending across all orders, focusing on those who have spent more than $500.

SQL Query for Data Extraction

To begin, let's take a look at our SQL query. This query joins the Customers and Orders tables, calculates the total spending for each customer, and filters for those who spent more than $500. It first joins the two tables by CustomerID, groups the data by customer details like ID, Name, Email, and Country, then sums up the total amount each customer spent. Finally, it filters out only those customers whose total spending exceeds $500. This approach gives us a focused dataset for further analysis.

Step 2: Connect to the Database in Python or R

Now that we have our query, the next step is to connect to the database and pull the data into Python or R, where we can load it into a DataFrame for analysis.

In **Python**, you can connect using the sqlite3 or SQLAlchemy libraries. With SQLAlchemy, establish a connection, execute the query, and load the result into a DataFrame. This makes it easy to work with the data directly in Python.

In **R**, use the DBI and RSQLite packages to connect to the database and run the query. After loading the results into a DataFrame, disconnect from the database. Now, you have a DataFrame called customer_data containing each customer's total spending, ready for manipulation.

Step 3: Data Manipulation in Python or R

With our data in place, let's start transforming it. We'll use Python's Pandas or R's dplyr package to classify customers into spending tiers, calculate summary statistics, and even create some visualizations.

Data Manipulation in Python with Pandas

1. **Classify Customers by Spending Tier**

   Using a simple function, we can assign customers into three spending tiers based on their total spending. For instance, customers spending over $1,000 might be classified as "High," over $750 as "Medium," and below that as "Low." By applying this function, we create a new column in the DataFrame labeled SpendingTier.

2. **Calculate Summary Statistics**

   Next, group the data by spending tier to calculate the average, total, and count of spending within each tier. This summary provides a quick overview of customer behavior across different spending levels.

3. **Visualize Spending by Tier**

   Finally, we can visualize the total spending by tier with a bar plot. Using Matplotlib, plot each spending tier along with its total spending, labeling the axes for clarity. This visualization makes it easy to see how spending compares across tiers.

Data Manipulation in R with dplyr

1. **Classify Customers by Spending Tier**

   In R, the mutate() and case_when() functions allow us

to create a new column for spending tiers. As in Python, we define thresholds for "High," "Medium," and "Low" tiers and apply them across the dataset.

2. **Calculate Summary Statistics**

   Use group_by() and summarize() to calculate average spending, total spending, and customer count by tier. This step provides the same summary statistics in a clean, easy-to-read format.

3. **Visualize Spending by Tier**

   For visualization, ggplot2 makes it easy to create a bar plot. Map the spending tiers to the x-axis and the total spending to the y-axis, and label the plot for clarity. This visual summary of spending by tier is a quick way to communicate customer behavior trends.

By following these steps, you'll have a clear, detailed breakdown of customer spending and behavior, and you'll be able to present these insights visually, making it easy to communicate your findings.

Step 4: Interpret and Analyze the Results

Now, let's analyze our results and see how combining SQL with Python or R enhances our insights:

- **Spending Tiers**: By categorizing customers into spending tiers, we gain a clearer picture of customer value segments, which is useful for targeted marketing. For example, "High" spending customers might be VIPs, while "Medium" spenders could be targeted for loyalty programs.
- **Summary Statistics**: The summary table provides insights into average and total spending for each tier, helping us understand the revenue contribution of each customer group.
- **Visualization**: The bar plot allows us to visually compare the spending across tiers, which is especially useful for sharing insights with stakeholders.

Conclusion: Combining SQL and Programming for Efficient Data Analysis

This example demonstrates how to extract data from a SQL database, manipulate it using Python or R, and visualize the results. Combining SQL and programming languages allows you to take advantage of SQL's power for data extraction and aggregation, along with Python or R's flexibility for data manipulation and visualization. This integrated workflow streamlines your analysis and provides a comprehensive approach to uncovering actionable insights.

By mastering these techniques, you can efficiently handle large datasets, perform sophisticated data transformations, and create impactful visualizations—all essential skills for intermediate-level data analytics.

Advanced Statistical Techniques for Insightful Analysis

Introduction to Key Techniques: Regression, Clustering, and Time Series Analysis

As you progress into intermediate data analytics, statistical techniques become essential tools for uncovering deeper insights and making data-driven predictions. This section introduces three foundational statistical methods— regression, clustering, and time series analysis—that are widely used across industries to understand patterns, segment data, and forecast future trends. Each of these techniques has unique applications and can provide powerful insights when applied appropriately.

1. Regression Analysis: Understanding Relationships and Making Predictions

Regression analysis is a statistical technique used to identify the relationship between one or more independent variables (predictors) and a dependent variable (outcome). It's particularly valuable for predictive modeling, as it allows analysts to understand how changes in predictor variables impact the outcome, helping in forecasting and decision-making.

Types of Regression

- **Linear Regression**: Linear regression is the simplest form of regression analysis, where the relationship between the independent variable(s) and the dependent variable is assumed to be linear. This method is widely used in business and economics for predictive analysis, such as forecasting sales or predicting housing prices based on factors like location and square footage.

- **Multiple Linear Regression**: Multiple linear regression is an extension of linear regression that involves multiple independent variables. For example, in predicting a house's price, factors like square footage, neighborhood, and age of the house can all be considered simultaneously. Multiple regression helps capture the impact of several predictors on the dependent variable, providing a more comprehensive model.

- **Logistic Regression**: Logistic regression is used when the dependent variable is binary or categorical, such as predicting whether a customer will churn (yes/no) based on their behavior. Logistic regression is commonly used in marketing and healthcare to predict outcomes where the response variable has two categories.

Practical Applications of Regression

- **Business Forecasting**: Regression is frequently used to forecast demand, sales, and revenue. For example, a company might use historical sales data to predict future sales based on factors such as seasonality, marketing spending, and economic indicators.

- **Healthcare Predictions**: In healthcare, regression models can help predict patient outcomes, such as the likelihood of readmission based on patient characteristics and medical history. This allows healthcare providers to allocate resources more efficiently.

- **Financial Risk Assessment**: Regression is also used in finance to assess risk, such as estimating credit risk based on income, debt, and credit history. This allows banks to make data-driven lending decisions.

Regression analysis provides a structured approach to understanding relationships within data and making informed predictions. By applying regression models, analysts can uncover trends, test hypotheses, and create predictive models that inform decision-making.

2. Clustering: Identifying Patterns and Segmentation

Clustering is an unsupervised learning technique that groups data into clusters, or segments, based on similarities among data points. Unlike regression, clustering doesn't predict an outcome but instead identifies natural groupings within the data. Clustering is highly valuable in exploratory data analysis, as it helps uncover hidden patterns, segment customers, and identify subgroups within a dataset.

Types of Clustering

- **K-Means Clustering**: K-means is one of the most popular clustering algorithms. It partitions data into K clusters based on the proximity of data points to cluster centroids. Analysts can define the number of clusters (K), and the algorithm assigns each data point to the nearest cluster. K-means is often used in customer segmentation and market research.

- **Hierarchical Clustering**: Hierarchical clustering builds a tree-like structure of clusters, where each data point is initially a single cluster, and similar clusters are merged iteratively. This method doesn't require specifying the number of clusters beforehand and is useful for exploring data hierarchies. Hierarchical clustering is used in fields like genomics to classify genetic data into meaningful categories.

- **DBSCAN (Density-Based Spatial Clustering of Applications with Noise)**: DBSCAN groups data points based on density, identifying clusters of various shapes and sizes. Unlike K-means, DBSCAN can identify outliers, which makes it suitable for datasets with noise or irregular patterns. It's commonly used in anomaly detection and geospatial analysis.

Practical Applications of Clustering

- **Customer Segmentation**: Clustering is widely used in marketing to segment customers based on purchasing behavior, demographics, and engagement. For example, customers can be grouped into segments like "high-value," "occasional," and "new" customers, allowing for targeted marketing strategies.
- **Image and Document Classification**: Clustering techniques are also used in machine learning for image and document classification. For instance, clustering can help organize large image databases by

grouping similar images or classifying documents based on topics.

- **Fraud Detection**: In finance, clustering can help detect unusual behavior that may indicate fraud. By clustering transaction data, banks can identify outliers or unusual patterns that deviate from typical customer behavior, flagging potential cases of fraud.

Clustering techniques provide a powerful way to explore data, identify patterns, and create targeted strategies based on natural groupings within the data. By segmenting data, analysts can gain insights that are not immediately apparent and create more personalized and effective strategies.

3. Time Series Analysis: Tracking Trends and Forecasting Over Time

Time series analysis is a statistical method used to analyze data points collected or recorded at specific time intervals. It's particularly valuable for identifying trends, seasonal patterns, and forecasting future values based on historical data. Time series analysis is widely used in fields that rely on trend data over time, such as economics, finance, and meteorology.

Key Components of Time Series Analysis

- **Trend**: A trend represents the long-term movement in a time series, showing the general direction of the data over time. For instance, sales data may exhibit an upward trend as a business grows.
- **Seasonality**: Seasonality refers to repeating patterns in the data at regular intervals, such as quarterly sales spikes in retail or increased electricity usage in winter. Identifying seasonal patterns is critical for understanding cyclic behaviors in data.
- **Cyclic Patterns**: Cyclic patterns are fluctuations that occur over a longer period than seasonality, often due to economic or business cycles. Unlike seasonality, cyclic patterns do not have a fixed frequency.
- **Noise**: Noise represents random fluctuations in the data that don't follow any specific pattern. Removing noise is essential for creating accurate forecasts.

Types of Time Series Models

- **Moving Average (MA)**: Moving average models smooth out short-term fluctuations by averaging values over a specific time window. This is useful for identifying trends and seasonality without the influence of noise.

- **Autoregressive Integrated Moving Average (ARIMA)**: ARIMA models are commonly used for forecasting time series data. ARIMA combines autoregressive (AR) and moving average (MA) components and is particularly effective for data with trends or seasonal patterns.

- **Seasonal Decomposition of Time Series (STL)**: STL is used to separate a time series into seasonal, trend, and residual components. This decomposition helps identify the underlying patterns and cyclical behaviors in data, making it easier to forecast accurately.

Practical Applications of Time Series Analysis

- **Sales Forecasting**: Time series analysis is frequently used in retail to forecast demand and sales. By identifying trends and seasonal patterns, companies can optimize inventory and marketing strategies to align with anticipated demand.

- **Financial Market Analysis**: In finance, time series models are used to analyze stock prices, interest rates, and exchange rates over time. Time series analysis helps investors understand market trends, volatility, and economic cycles, aiding in investment decisions.

- **Weather and Environmental Forecasting**: Meteorologists use time series models to predict weather patterns, such as temperature and rainfall, based on historical data. These models also apply to environmental monitoring, such as tracking pollution levels over time.

Time series analysis enables analysts to gain insights into trends, patterns, and forecasts, allowing for data-driven decision-making that anticipates future events. This technique is invaluable for industries that depend on timely, accurate forecasts.

Conclusion: The Power of Advanced Statistical Techniques

Regression, clustering, and time series analysis are key techniques that elevate your ability to derive insights from data. By applying regression, you can understand relationships and make predictions. With clustering, you can identify natural groupings and segments, allowing for targeted actions based on patterns. Time series analysis lets you forecast trends, helping organizations prepare for future demand and changes. Together, these statistical methods form a powerful toolkit for intermediate data analysts, enabling you to analyze data in-depth and make impactful, data-driven decisions.

Choosing the Right Method: A Decision-Making Guide for Statistical Analysis

With a variety of statistical techniques available, choosing the right method for data analysis can be challenging. Each technique has specific strengths, requirements, and applications. To help you make informed decisions, this guide provides a structured approach for selecting the most appropriate method based on the nature of your data, the relationships you want to explore, and the outcomes you aim to predict.

This guide focuses on three main types of analysis techniques: regression, clustering, and time series analysis. We'll cover how to decide which method to use, when it's best suited, and what types of data each technique requires.

Step 1: Define Your Data Type and Analysis Goal

The first step in choosing the right statistical technique is to understand the type of data you have and the goal of your analysis. Answering the following questions can clarify your path:

1. **Is the data continuous or categorical?**
   - Continuous data includes variables that can take on a range of values, such as income, temperature, and age.
   - Categorical data includes variables that fall into distinct groups, such as gender, region, or product category.
2. **Do you want to understand relationships, make predictions, or segment the data?**

- Understand relationships: If your goal is to understand how one variable influences another, regression might be the right choice.
- Make predictions: If you aim to predict future outcomes based on historical data, regression and time series analysis are common choices.
- Segment the data: If you want to group similar data points or create distinct segments, clustering is likely the best approach.

Once you've clarified your data type and analysis goal, you can proceed to select the most suitable technique.

Step 2: Determine When to Use Regression Analysis

Regression is appropriate when your primary goal is to understand relationships between variables or predict the value of a target variable based on one or more predictors.

Best Suited For:

- **Continuous Outcome Variables**: Regression is ideal when the outcome you're trying to predict is continuous, like sales revenue, temperature, or customer spending.

- **Explaining Relationships**: Use regression when you want to quantify the relationship between predictor and outcome variables. For example, you may want to understand how marketing spend affects sales or how age impacts income levels.

Common Applications of Regression Analysis

- **Linear Regression**: Use linear regression if you're analyzing a single predictor variable with a linear relationship to the outcome, like predicting house prices based on square footage.
- **Multiple Linear Regression**: Choose multiple linear regression when you have multiple predictors. For instance, predicting a product's sales could consider factors such as advertising budget, season, and competitor pricing.
- **Logistic Regression**: Opt for logistic regression if your outcome variable is binary (e.g., yes/no or 0/1), such as predicting customer churn or email response likelihood.

Example Decision Scenarios

- **Sales Prediction**: If you want to predict next month's sales based on factors like past sales, advertising spend, and economic indicators, multiple linear regression is a good choice.
- **Customer Churn**: If you're predicting whether a customer will churn based on account activity and demographics, logistic regression is ideal due to the binary outcome.

Use regression analysis when your goal is to make predictions or understand linear relationships, especially when your outcome variable is continuous or binary.

Step 3: Decide If Clustering is Appropriate for Your Needs

Clustering is a type of unsupervised learning that's ideal when you want to segment data into groups without predefined categories. Clustering does not have a dependent variable; instead, it looks for patterns or similarities within the data.

Best Suited For:

- **Exploratory Data Analysis**: Clustering is highly effective for exploring data and discovering hidden patterns, such as grouping customers by purchasing behavior.
- **Segmentation Without Predefined Labels**: Use clustering when you want to categorize data points (e.g., customers, products, or transactions) into groups based on similarity, especially when you don't have predefined labels.

Common Applications of Clustering

- **K-Means Clustering**: Use K-means when you know the approximate number of clusters you want, such as customer segments in marketing.
- **Hierarchical Clustering**: Choose hierarchical clustering if you want a tree-like structure to visualize relationships, which can help you identify sub-clusters within larger groups.

- **DBSCAN**: Select DBSCAN for data with irregular cluster shapes or significant noise, as it can identify clusters of various densities.

Example Decision Scenarios

- **Customer Segmentation**: If your goal is to segment customers based on purchasing behavior, K-means clustering can group them into categories like "high spenders" or "infrequent buyers."
- **Anomaly Detection**: If you want to identify unusual transactions, DBSCAN can help by separating common patterns from anomalies.

Use clustering when your analysis involves grouping data points without a dependent variable, especially when you need to explore and identify patterns in the data.

Step 4: Choose Time Series Analysis for Temporal Data

Time series analysis is designed for data that is collected over time. It's ideal for analyzing trends, seasonality, and cyclic patterns in data that changes at regular intervals, such as daily, monthly, or annually.

Best Suited For:

- **Forecasting Future Values**: Use time series analysis if your primary goal is to forecast future trends based on past data.
- **Analyzing Patterns Over Time**: Time series analysis is effective for identifying patterns, such as trends (long-term movement), seasonality (regular fluctuations), and cycles (longer, irregular patterns).

Common Applications of Time Series Analysis

- **Moving Averages**: Use moving averages to smooth out short-term fluctuations and reveal underlying trends in time series data.
- **ARIMA (Autoregressive Integrated Moving Average)**: Choose ARIMA when you need a comprehensive model for forecasting that can handle both trend and seasonality.
- **Exponential Smoothing**: Use exponential smoothing for data with a strong trend or seasonal

component, especially when recent observations are more relevant to the forecast.

Example Decision Scenarios

- **Sales Forecasting**: If you want to predict future sales based on historical data, such as monthly sales figures, ARIMA or exponential smoothing is ideal.
- **Weather Forecasting**: If your data includes daily or monthly temperature readings, time series analysis can help identify seasonal trends and forecast future temperatures.

Use time series analysis when your data includes a time component and you need to analyze trends, seasonal patterns, or cycles over time.

Final Decision Guide: Putting It All Together

If your primary goal is prediction or understanding relationships between variables, use regression.

If you need to explore patterns or segment data without predefined categories, clustering is your best choice.

If your data is time-based and you need to analyze trends or make future projections, go with time series analysis.

By following this decision-making guide, you'll be able to choose the statistical method that best fits your data and analysis goals. Each technique offers unique insights and can drive impactful data-driven decisions when applied to the right type of data. As you continue to master these techniques, you'll gain the flexibility to select the optimal approach for any data analysis challenge, enhancing the depth and quality of your insights.

Case Study: Analyzing Customer Churn in a Subscription-Based Business

In this case study, we'll explore a mini-project focused on understanding customer churn in a subscription-based business. Customer churn—the rate at which customers stop using a service—is a critical metric for businesses with recurring revenue models. High churn can negatively impact revenue, so identifying the factors contributing to churn can help a company take proactive steps to retain customers.

The goal of this project is to:

1. Retrieve customer and subscription data from a SQL database.
2. Process and clean the data in Python or R.
3. Use logistic regression to model churn and identify key factors associated with customers leaving the service.

Step 1: Retrieve Data from a SQL Database

The database contains two tables:

- **Customers**: Information about each customer, including CustomerID, SignupDate, Country, Age, and Gender.
- **Subscriptions**: Information about each subscription, including SubscriptionID, CustomerID, SubscriptionDate, Churned (Yes/No), and MonthlySpend.

Our goal is to retrieve data that allows us to explore customer demographics and subscription details to identify churn patterns.

SQL Query to Extract Data

We'll start by joining the **Customers** and **Subscriptions** tables on the CustomerID, filtering for customers who have had at least six months of subscription history. This helps us avoid including new customers who might not have been with the service long enough to decide if they want to stay or leave.

SQL Query for Data Extraction

Let's start by constructing our SQL query to bring together customer demographics and subscription details. Here, we join the Customers and Subscriptions tables on CustomerID to combine these insights. Additionally, we use the DATEDIFF function to filter for customers who signed up at least six months ago. This query effectively prepares a dataset for further analysis by ensuring we only work with established customers.

Step 2: Load and Process the Data in Python or R

Once the query is ready, the next step is loading this data into either Python or R, where we can process it further.

In **Python**, we connect to the database using the SQLAlchemy library, run the SQL query, and load the results into a DataFrame. This makes the data readily accessible for cleaning and analysis.

In **R**, we use DBI and RSQLite to connect, execute the query, and load the results into a DataFrame. After finishing, we disconnect from the database. With our data now in a DataFrame called df, we're ready to start the cleaning and transformation process.

Step 3: Data Cleaning and Feature Engineering

Now that we have our dataset, it's time to clean and prepare it for analysis. Here's a breakdown of the main steps:

1. **Convert Date Columns**
   We convert the SignupDate and SubscriptionDate columns into datetime formats to make date-based calculations easier.
2. **Calculate Subscription Duration**
   Next, we calculate the number of months since each customer signed up, giving us an idea of how long each has been with the service.

3. **Encode Categorical Variables**
   Finally, we convert categorical variables like Country and Gender into numerical values, using one-hot encoding in Python or binary encoding in R. This step is essential for running predictive models effectively.

Data Cleaning and Feature Engineering in Python

In Python, we use Pandas to convert date columns, calculate subscription duration, and apply one-hot encoding to categorical variables. These transformations help make the dataset model-ready.

Data Cleaning and Feature Engineering in R

In R, we achieve the same results using lubridate for date transformations and dplyr for data manipulation. The mutate function helps us create new features, while one-hot encoding allows us to handle categorical data.

Step 4: Apply Logistic Regression to Model Churn

With our cleaned and transformed data, we're ready to apply logistic regression. This model is ideal for predicting binary outcomes, like whether a customer will churn (1) or stay (0).

Logistic Regression in Python

In Python, we use scikit-learn to split our data into training and testing sets, train a logistic regression model, and evaluate its performance. By defining features and the target variable, we can train the model on one part of the data and test its predictions on another. Metrics like accuracy and classification reports give insight into the model's effectiveness.

Logistic Regression in R

In R, we use caret to split the data, train a logistic regression model, and evaluate its predictions. After fitting the model, we use the predict function to generate predictions, setting a threshold to classify results. Finally, a confusion matrix provides an accuracy measure, helping us understand the model's predictive power.

Through these steps, we've taken raw data, prepared it for analysis, and used logistic regression to predict customer churn. This process not only aids in customer retention strategies but also demonstrates how SQL, Python, and R can work together to turn data into actionable insights.

Step 5: Interpret and Analyze the Results

After running the logistic regression, you can analyze the output to understand which features significantly impact customer churn.

- **Feature Importance**: By examining the coefficients in the logistic regression model, you can identify the factors most associated with churn. For example, a higher SubscriptionDuration might indicate a reduced likelihood of churn, while customers with higher MonthlySpend may have a lower risk of leaving.
- **Model Accuracy**: Assess the model's accuracy to determine how well it predicts churn. You can use metrics like accuracy score, precision, recall, and F1-score to evaluate performance.

- **Recommendations**: Based on the insights, you might recommend targeted retention strategies. For instance, customers with shorter subscription durations might benefit from engagement campaigns, while those with lower monthly spending might respond to upsell opportunities.

Conclusion: Applying Advanced Statistical Techniques to Business Challenges

This case study demonstrates how to integrate SQL, Python or R, and logistic regression to analyze customer churn. By retrieving data from a database, processing it in a programming environment, and applying statistical modeling, you gain valuable insights into customer behavior that can directly inform business strategy. Through this hands-on project, you've learned how to leverage data analytics tools to solve real-world business problems—an essential skill set for any intermediate data analyst.

Integrating Skills for Real-World Data Analysis

Connecting Theory to Practice: Real-World Scenarios Requiring Databases, Programming, and Statistics

As data analytics evolves, so does the need for multifaceted skill sets that can address complex problems. In the real world, data analysts often work with massive datasets stored in databases, transform and analyze these data using programming, and apply statistical models to uncover insights that drive decision-making. This section explores real-world scenarios across various industries where the combined use of databases, programming, and statistics is essential for effective data analysis.

By understanding how these skills interact, you'll be better prepared to bridge the gap between theory and practice, turning your technical knowledge into actionable insights that can solve business challenges.

1. E-commerce: Customer Lifetime Value Analysis

In e-commerce, understanding customer lifetime value (CLV) is crucial for optimizing marketing spend, personalizing promotions, and forecasting revenue. Calculating CLV requires the integration of databases, programming, and statistical methods.

Step-by-Step Application

- **Databases**: CLV analysis begins with retrieving data on customer transactions, demographics, and purchase history from a database. This may involve joining multiple tables (such as customers, orders, and products) to get a comprehensive view of each customer's purchase behavior.
- **Programming**: After extracting data, programming languages like Python or R are used to clean, transform, and analyze the data. Using libraries such as Pandas in Python, analysts can calculate the total amount spent per customer, purchase frequency, and recency of purchases.
- **Statistics**: Finally, statistical techniques such as regression analysis or predictive modeling can forecast the CLV based on historical purchase

behavior. For instance, logistic regression might be used to model the probability of repeat purchases, while a predictive model can estimate the future spending of each customer.

Real-World Impact

This integrated approach allows e-commerce businesses to predict which customers are likely to bring high value over time. With these insights, companies can create targeted marketing strategies, allocate resources efficiently, and enhance customer retention.

2. Healthcare: Predicting Patient Readmissions

In healthcare, hospitals and clinics strive to reduce patient readmissions, which can indicate issues with patient care quality and increase operational costs. Predicting patient readmissions requires combining data from electronic health records (EHR), programming skills to process this data, and statistical models to predict readmission risks.

Step-by-Step Application

- **Databases**: Patient data, including demographic information, medical history, treatment details, and previous admissions, is stored in EHR databases. SQL is typically used to retrieve relevant data, joining tables with patient records, admissions, and treatment codes.
- **Programming**: Python or R is used to preprocess the data. This might involve handling missing values, encoding categorical variables (e.g., treatment types), and calculating derived features (e.g., the time since the last admission). Libraries like Pandas in Python and dplyr in R make it easier to transform data into a format suitable for analysis.
- **Statistics**: Predictive models, such as logistic regression or machine learning classifiers, can help predict the likelihood of readmission based on historical data. These models may use variables like patient age, diagnosis, length of stay, and treatment plan to assess readmission risks.

Real-World Impact

By identifying patients at high risk of readmission, healthcare providers can take preventive measures, such as personalized follow-ups or improved discharge planning, to reduce readmission rates. This not only improves patient care but also reduces healthcare costs and enhances hospital efficiency.

3. Retail: Inventory Optimization and Demand Forecasting

Inventory optimization is a common challenge in retail, where businesses need to balance stock levels to meet demand without overstocking. Demand forecasting requires integrating databases (for sales data), programming (for data processing), and statistical methods (for trend and seasonality analysis).

Step-by-Step Application

- **Databases**: Inventory and sales data are typically stored in relational databases. Using SQL, analysts can retrieve historical sales data by product, location, and date. They might also pull data on seasonal promotions, discounts, and stock levels.

- **Programming**: Python or R is used to clean and prepare the data for forecasting. Data transformations might include calculating moving averages, smoothing fluctuations, and normalizing sales figures. Python libraries like Pandas and NumPy, or R packages like dplyr, make it easier to handle these operations.
- **Statistics**: Time series analysis, using methods such as ARIMA (Autoregressive Integrated Moving Average) or exponential smoothing, can forecast future demand based on historical sales patterns. These models help identify trends and seasonality, which are crucial for optimizing inventory.

Real-World Impact

Accurate demand forecasting enables retailers to maintain optimal inventory levels, ensuring that popular items are available when needed while minimizing excess stock. This reduces storage costs, improves cash flow, and enhances customer satisfaction by preventing stockouts.

4. Finance: Credit Risk Assessment

In finance, credit risk assessment is vital for determining the likelihood that a borrower will default on a loan. Financial institutions rely on data-driven insights to make lending decisions, requiring the integration of databases, programming, and statistical modeling.

Step-by-Step Application

- **Databases**: Credit history, transaction data, and borrower demographics are stored in financial databases. SQL queries can be used to retrieve relevant data, such as income, employment history, credit score, and existing debt, from various tables.

- **Programming**: After extracting the data, Python or R is used to preprocess it. This might include handling missing values, transforming variables (e.g., normalizing income levels), and generating new features, such as debt-to-income ratio. Programming also allows for exploratory data analysis to better understand patterns in credit behavior.

- **Statistics**: Logistic regression or machine learning models, such as decision trees or random forests, are used to predict the probability of default. These models use multiple predictors—such as credit score, income, and past defaults—to estimate risk levels and assign a risk score to each borrower.

Real-World Impact

By accurately assessing credit risk, financial institutions can make more informed lending decisions, reduce the risk of loan defaults, and optimize interest rates. This ensures a healthier loan portfolio and minimizes financial losses.

5. Marketing: Campaign Performance Analysis and Customer Segmentation

Marketing teams often analyze campaign performance and segment customers to deliver personalized experiences. This analysis requires data from multiple sources, programming for data transformation, and statistical techniques for segmentation and performance measurement.

Step-by-Step Application

- **Databases**: Data on customer demographics, interactions, and purchases is stored in marketing databases. SQL is used to pull together relevant data from multiple tables, such as customer profiles, campaign touchpoints, and purchase history.

- **Programming**: Python or R is used to preprocess the data, which may include aggregating metrics (e.g., total purchases by customer) and calculating engagement scores (e.g., email opens or website visits). One-hot encoding can be applied to categorical variables like customer preferences.

- **Statistics**: Clustering techniques, such as K-means clustering, are used to segment customers based on characteristics like age, spending habits, and engagement. Additionally, A/B testing or statistical tests like chi-square tests can evaluate the effectiveness of different campaign strategies.

Real-World Impact

Customer segmentation allows marketers to create targeted campaigns, ensuring that messaging resonates with specific customer groups. Campaign performance analysis helps optimize future marketing spend, resulting in higher engagement, conversion rates, and customer satisfaction.

6. Public Health: Disease Outbreak Prediction and Control

In public health, predicting and managing disease outbreaks is essential to prevent the spread of infectious diseases. This requires analyzing data from health records, using programming for data processing, and applying statistical models to forecast trends and hotspots.

Step-by-Step Application

- **Databases**: Data on patient cases, demographics, and geographical locations is stored in health databases. SQL is used to extract relevant data on reported cases, including the time and location of each case, as well as demographic details.
- **Programming**: Python or R is used to clean the data, calculate the rate of new cases, and create derived features, such as population density in affected areas. Spatial data processing can also be performed to link case data with geographical information.
- **Statistics**: Time series analysis or predictive models, such as logistic regression, can forecast future case

counts and identify hotspots. These models may take into account seasonality and environmental factors (e.g., temperature or humidity) that influence disease spread.

Real-World Impact

Disease outbreak prediction helps public health officials allocate resources efficiently, inform the public, and implement control measures, such as vaccination campaigns or travel restrictions, to mitigate the spread of disease.

Conclusion: The Power of Integrating Databases, Programming, and Statistics

In each of these scenarios, the combined use of databases, programming, and statistics allows data analysts to tackle real-world challenges effectively. By integrating data retrieval (SQL), data transformation (Python or R), and statistical modeling, analysts can uncover actionable insights that directly impact decision-making.

As you continue to develop these skills, you'll be better prepared to handle complex data projects and drive meaningful results in various industries. This integration of skills empowers you to move beyond theory, applying data analytics to solve practical, impactful problems in the real world.

Practice Exercise: Customer Purchase Behavior Analysis

In this structured practice exercise, you will assume the role of a data analyst for an online retail company. Your task is to analyze customer purchasing behavior to help the marketing team understand spending patterns, identify high-value customers, and explore potential insights for targeted marketing. This exercise will guide you through retrieving data from a SQL database, cleaning and transforming it using Python or R, and presenting your findings in a professional report.

By the end of this exercise, you will have a synthesized view of how databases, programming, and statistical techniques can be combined for real-world data analysis.

Scenario Overview

The online retail company wants to gain insights into customer purchase behavior to enhance customer loyalty and improve marketing strategies. They are particularly interested in understanding:

1. Which customers spend the most on the platform.
2. How customer demographics (e.g., age and location) relate to spending patterns.
3. Seasonal trends in purchasing behavior.

The dataset you'll work with consists of two tables in a SQL database:

1. **Customers**: Contains information on each customer, including CustomerID, Name, Age, Country, and SignupDate.
2. **Orders**: Contains details on each order, including OrderID, CustomerID, OrderDate, and TotalAmount.

Instructions

Step 1: Retrieve Data from the SQL Database

Your first task is to connect to the SQL database and retrieve relevant data from the **Customers** and **Orders** tables. You'll need to perform a join to merge customer demographics with their order history.

SQL Query to Retrieve Data

First, we'll write an SQL query to pull key information about customers and their orders. We want to retrieve the CustomerID, Name, Age, Country, and SignupDate from the Customers table, along with the OrderID, OrderDate, and TotalAmount from the Orders table. We'll focus only on customers who have made at least one purchase by joining these tables on the CustomerID. This query gives us a combined dataset of customer demographics and order details, ready for deeper analysis.

Step 2: Load Data into Python or R

Once the data is retrieved, the next step is loading it into either Python or R for further manipulation.

In **Python**, use pandas and SQLAlchemy to connect to the database, run the query, and load the results into a

DataFrame. This DataFrame will serve as the foundation for further analysis.

In **R**, connect with the DBI and dplyr libraries, execute the SQL query, and load the results into a DataFrame. After that, disconnect from the database. Now, our data is in a DataFrame called df in both Python and R, making it accessible for cleaning and transformation.

Step 3: Data Cleaning and Transformation

With the data in place, let's clean and prepare it to make it analysis-ready:

1. **Handle Missing Values**
   First, check for any missing values. Decide whether to fill these gaps (perhaps with averages) or remove them to ensure consistent data quality.
2. **Convert Date Columns**
   Convert OrderDate and SignupDate into date formats, which allows you to extract useful information like the year and month for time-based analysis.
3. **Calculate Total Spending per Customer**
   Group the data by CustomerID and calculate the total

spending for each customer, then add this as a new column, TotalSpent.

4. **Create Age Groups**
   To understand spending by demographics, categorize customers into age groups (like 18-25, 26-35, etc.).

Data Cleaning and Transformation in Python

In Python, use Pandas to check for missing values, convert dates, calculate total spending, and create age groups. This setup allows for easy analysis on customer behavior.

Data Cleaning and Transformation in R

In R, use dplyr and lubridate for similar transformations. With mutate, you can create age groups and add calculated columns, ensuring the data is ready for further insights.

Step 4: Analysis

With the cleaned data, we're ready to perform some meaningful analyses:

1. **Top 10 High-Value Customers**
   Identify the top 10 customers based on total spending.

This list provides insight into your most valuable customers by showing their CustomerID, Name, and TotalSpent.

2. **Spending by Age Group**
   Calculate the average total spent by each age group. This helps pinpoint which demographics contribute most to revenue.

3. **Monthly Sales Trend**
   Analyze monthly sales by aggregating TotalAmount by OrderDate, grouped by year and month. This allows you to identify seasonal trends in purchasing behavior, which can inform marketing and inventory strategies.

Analysis in Python

In Python, use Pandas to identify top customers, calculate average spending by age group, and analyze monthly sales trends. This setup provides a structured way to view customer behavior and sales patterns.

Analysis in R

In R, use dplyr for grouping and summarizing data, and ggplot2 (if needed) for visualizing the monthly sales trend. This analysis brings clarity to customer spending habits and trends over time.

By following these steps, you'll gain valuable insights into customer behavior, age-based spending, and monthly sales trends, providing a solid foundation for data-driven decisions.

Step 5: Report Findings

Write a professional report that includes the following sections:

1. **Introduction**: Briefly describe the purpose of the analysis.
2. **Methodology**: Summarize how data was retrieved, cleaned, and analyzed.
3. **Findings**:
   - **Top 10 High-Value Customers**: List customer details and total spending.
   - **Spending by Age Group**: Describe which age groups are the most valuable.

- o **Monthly Sales Trend**: Show seasonal patterns or trends in customer spending.
4. **Conclusion**: Summarize insights and suggest potential actions, such as targeted marketing campaigns for high-value age groups or timing promotions during high-spending months.

Sample Report Excerpt

Introduction

This report analyzes customer purchasing behavior to provide insights into high-value customers, spending trends by age group, and monthly sales patterns. The purpose of this analysis is to support the marketing team in identifying target customer segments and optimizing promotional strategies.

Methodology

Data was retrieved from the company's SQL database, containing information on customer demographics and order details. The data was cleaned, transformed, and analyzed using Python/R, focusing on calculating total spending per customer, average spending by age group, and monthly sales trends.

Findings

- **Top 10 High-Value Customers**: The top 10 customers accounted for a significant portion of total revenue, with each spending an average of $X.
- **Spending by Age Group**: The 26-35 age group showed the highest average spending, indicating potential for targeted marketing.
- **Monthly Sales Trend**: Sales peaked in November and December, suggesting a seasonal trend tied to holiday shopping.

Conclusion

The analysis highlights the importance of targeting the 26-35 age group and planning marketing campaigns around high-spending months. Additional analysis could explore specific products purchased by high-value customers for more focused marketing.

This structured exercise combines database querying, data manipulation, statistical analysis, and report writing. It provides a complete workflow that synthesizes the skills covered in this chapter, giving you hands-on experience with real-world data analysis and preparing you for similar projects in a professional setting.

End-of-Chapter Summary and Key Takeaways

Recap Key Points

In this chapter, we delved into the essential components of intermediate data analytics, building on foundational knowledge to equip you with advanced skills. Here's a summary of the main techniques and concepts we explored, with an emphasis on how they go beyond beginner-level approaches:

1. **Databases as the Core of Data Storage and Retrieval**:
   o **Advanced SQL Queries**: We introduced complex SQL queries, including joins, subqueries, and window functions, that allow you to retrieve and manipulate data from

multiple tables efficiently. These techniques are essential for handling relational data at scale, unlike basic SELECT queries that only retrieve simple data views.

2. **Programming for Data Manipulation and Analysis**:

   ○ **Key Libraries in Python and R**: We discussed intermediate libraries like Pandas and NumPy in Python, and dplyr and ggplot2 in R, which enable data manipulation and visualization at a level of complexity beyond basic spreadsheets.

   ○ **Data Transformation and Cleaning**: You learned how to apply functions and chains to filter, aggregate, and reshape data, preparing it for analysis. Unlike beginner approaches that rely on manual cleaning or limited tools, programming offers automation and efficiency for large datasets.

3. **Advanced Statistical Techniques for Insightful Analysis**:

   ○ **Regression, Clustering, and Time Series Analysis**: We explored statistical methods that enable deeper insights into data. Regression helps understand relationships and predict outcomes, clustering uncovers patterns within data, and time series analysis reveals trends over time. These techniques are crucial for identifying actionable insights, as opposed to basic descriptive statistics.

4. **Integrating Skills for Real-World Data Analysis**:

   o **Connecting Theory to Practice**: Through real-world scenarios and a structured practice exercise, you learned how to combine databases, programming, and statistics for comprehensive data analysis. This integration prepares you for real-world projects where multiple skills are required to extract meaningful insights and communicate findings effectively.

Challenge Questions

To reinforce the concepts covered in this chapter, here are some thought-provoking questions designed to encourage critical thinking and practical application. Try to answer these questions based on the techniques you've learned, and consider how each approach would apply to real-world situations.

1. **Advanced SQL and Data Retrieval**
   - When analyzing a large dataset stored in multiple tables, how would you decide which type of join (INNER JOIN, LEFT JOIN, etc.) is most appropriate for your analysis? Can you think of a scenario where using a LEFT JOIN would provide insights that an INNER JOIN would miss?
   - Imagine you're tasked with retrieving the most recent purchase for each customer from a database. What SQL techniques could you use to accomplish this efficiently?

2. **Programming for Data Manipulation**
   - When working with a dataset that includes missing values, how would you decide between removing the rows, filling them with averages, or applying other imputation techniques? What factors would influence your decision?

o Suppose you have a dataset with thousands of rows and want to create a new feature based on multiple existing columns. What programming techniques could you use to streamline this process, and how would they improve efficiency compared to manual calculations?

3. **Statistical Techniques for Analysis**

   o If you're tasked with predicting customer churn for a subscription service, how would you decide whether regression or a clustering approach would be more appropriate? Under what conditions might you use both methods in the same project?

   o Imagine you are analyzing seasonal sales trends for a retailer. How would you decide whether to use a time series model (e.g., ARIMA) or another approach like moving averages? What factors, such as seasonality or cyclic patterns, would you consider in your analysis?

4. **Integrating Skills for Real-World Data Analysis**

   o Consider a scenario where you're working with a SQL database, Python/R for data manipulation, and a statistical model for analysis. How would you organize your workflow to ensure data accuracy and maintain a smooth transition between each stage?

o   Reflecting on the practice exercise from this chapter, how would you communicate your findings to a non-technical audience, such as a marketing or business team? What elements would you focus on to make your analysis understandable and actionable?

5. **Practical Applications and Future Exploration**

o   How could you apply the techniques in this chapter to a field outside of business, such as public health, education, or environmental science? For instance, how might clustering or regression be used to solve problems unique to these fields?

o   Looking ahead, what additional skills or tools do you think would be useful to continue advancing in data analytics? Are there areas from this chapter you'd like to explore more deeply, such as machine learning techniques for predictive analysis or advanced SQL optimizations?

Final Thoughts

This chapter introduced you to intermediate data analytics techniques that go beyond basic analysis, equipping you with the skills to handle real-world data challenges. By combining databases, programming, and statistics, you're now better prepared to tackle complex datasets, extract valuable insights, and present your findings in a meaningful way.

As you move forward in your data analytics journey, continue practicing these techniques, experimenting with different approaches, and seeking opportunities to apply your skills in new contexts. With each project, you'll gain confidence in selecting the right tools, interpreting results accurately, and making data-driven decisions that can have a real impact.

Chapter 2: Advanced SQL Techniques for Data Analysts

Enhancing Data Retrieval Skills

Complex Joins and Nested Queries

In this section, we'll explore advanced SQL join techniques and nested queries. These techniques are essential for handling complex data retrieval tasks, where basic joins or single-layer queries won't suffice. We'll cover FULL OUTER JOIN, SELF JOIN, and nested queries, each with examples to help illustrate their usefulness.

By mastering these skills, you'll be able to combine data across multiple tables and extract multi-layered information, helping you answer detailed and complex questions from your database.

FULL OUTER JOIN

Let's start with the FULL OUTER JOIN. This type of join is useful when you want to retrieve all records from two tables, including any records that don't have matching rows in the other table. In a FULL OUTER JOIN, if there's no match in one table, the columns from that table will have NULL values for those rows.

Imagine you have two tables: **Customers** and **Orders**. The **Customers** table lists all your customers, and the **Orders** table shows each customer's orders. Now, if you want to see all customers along with their orders—even if some customers haven't placed any orders, and some orders don't have a matching customer ID—you'd use a FULL OUTER JOIN.

Here's how the SQL query works. In this example, we're selecting the CustomerID and Name from the Customers table, along with OrderID and OrderDate from the Orders table, using a FULL OUTER JOIN to bring in all rows from both tables. If a customer hasn't placed an order, their details will still appear, with NULL values in the order columns. Similarly, if there's an order without a matching customer, the customer details will show as NULL. Essentially, a FULL OUTER JOIN gives you a complete view of both tables, showing all data regardless of matches.

Now let's talk about the SELF JOIN. A SELF JOIN is simply when a table joins with itself. This is useful when you need to compare rows within the same table. Imagine you have a table called Employees with columns for EmployeeID, Name, and ManagerID, where ManagerID represents the ID of each employee's manager. To create a list that pairs each employee with their manager's name, you would use a SELF JOIN. In this query, we're using the Employees table twice with two different aliases—e1 for the employee and e2 for the manager. By joining e1.ManagerID with e2.EmployeeID, we can pair each employee with their manager, displaying both names. The SELF JOIN is a great tool when you need to relate rows within the same table, such as connecting employees to their managers.

Lastly, let's explore nested queries, or subqueries, which are queries within queries. They're ideal when you need to perform multiple steps to get the desired data. For example, suppose you want to find customers who have spent more than the average amount on their orders. To do this, you'd first calculate the average order amount, and then use that result in another query to filter customers. This is where a nested query comes in handy. Here, we're selecting

CustomerID and Name from the Customers table, but only for customers whose total spending exceeds the average order amount.

Let's break this down. The **inner query** calculates the average order amount. Then, in the **middle query**, we group the orders by CustomerID and use **HAVING** to filter for customers whose total spending is above this average. Finally, the **outer query** selects the customer details for those customers.

Nested queries allow you to layer your logic, making it possible to perform complex filtering and calculations that wouldn't be possible with a single query alone.

Combining Techniques

Let's look at a quick example of how these techniques can be combined in a real-world scenario.

Imagine you're analyzing sales data for a retail company. You want to:

1. Retrieve all customers and their orders.

2. List employees and their managers.

3. Find customers who have spent above average.

You could use a FULL OUTER JOIN to view all customers and orders, a SELF JOIN to list employees and their managers, and a nested query to find high-spending customers.

Together, these techniques give you powerful ways to handle complex data retrieval tasks, providing a comprehensive view of your data.

In this section, we covered some advanced SQL techniques for data retrieval, including FULL OUTER JOIN, SELF JOIN, and nested queries. These techniques expand your ability to work with data from multiple tables, perform self-referencing joins, and layer queries for complex filtering.

By mastering complex joins and nested queries, you'll be better prepared to handle sophisticated data requests and unlock deeper insights from your database. These skills will allow you to tackle real-world data challenges with confidence.

Window Functions for Statistical Analysis

In this section, we'll explore SQL window functions, powerful tools for performing calculations across sets of rows related to the current row. Unlike regular aggregate functions that summarize data and collapse rows, window functions keep each row in your result set intact while adding new insights alongside it.

We'll cover some of the most commonly used window functions—**ROW_NUMBER, RANK, LEAD**, and **LAG**—and provide practical examples of how to use them in real-world scenarios, like tracking trends and performing time-based analysis.

Understanding Window Functions

Window functions calculate values over a set of rows, known as the "window," that are related to the current row. The window can be based on partitions or specific orderings, allowing you to compare data across different segments or track changes over time. Window functions are valuable when you need to analyze data trends, rank data, or access values from previous or subsequent rows without collapsing the result set.

ROW_NUMBER: Assigning a Sequence to Each Row

Let's start with **ROW_NUMBER**. The **ROW_NUMBER** function assigns a unique number to each row within a partition. This is helpful when you want to create a sequence for rows within a certain group, like ranking orders by date for each customer.

Imagine you have an Orders table with columns for CustomerID, OrderID, and OrderDate, and you want to assign a row number to each order for every customer, sorted by the date of the order. You can use the ROW_NUMBER function to accomplish this. Here's how it works: by using PARTITION BY CustomerID, we create a unique numbering sequence for each customer, and ORDER BY OrderDate ensures the orders are arranged by date within each customer's sequence. This query will return each order with an additional column called OrderSequence, which numbers each order chronologically for every customer. This approach is especially helpful when you want to review each customer's order history in the sequence they made their purchases.

Now, let's look at the RANK function, which is similar to ROW_NUMBER but designed to handle ties. When multiple rows have the same value in the column used for ordering, RANK assigns the same rank to those rows and skips the following rank. For instance, imagine you're working with a table called EmployeeSales, which contains columns for EmployeeID, SalesAmount, and Department. You want to rank employees within each department based on their sales. Here, PARTITION BY Department divides the data by department, and ORDER BY SalesAmount DESC ranks employees in each department from the highest to the lowest sales. RANK is ideal when you need to consider ties in your ranking, providing a fair representation even when multiple employees have the same sales figures.

In this query:

- **PARTITION BY Department** creates separate rankings for each department.

- **ORDER BY SalesAmount DESC** ranks employees from highest to lowest sales within each department.

If two employees have the same sales amount, they'll receive the same rank. For example, if two employees have the highest sales in their department, they'll both be ranked 1, and the next employee will be ranked 3. **RANK** is useful when you need to handle ties, like ranking top performers in each department or identifying top products in each category.

LEAD and LAG: Accessing Next and Previous Rows

LEAD and **LAG** are window functions that allow you to look at the values in the next row or previous row within a specific window. These functions are extremely useful for time-based analysis, where you might want to compare a value with the previous or next period.

Imagine you're working with a **MonthlySales** table that includes **Month, ProductID**, and **SalesAmount**. You want to compare each month's sales with the sales from the previous month for each product. To do this, you can use **LAG** to access the previous month's sales amount.

Here's how the query works. We're selecting the Month, ProductID, and SalesAmount from the MonthlySales table, and we're adding a new column that shows the sales amount from the previous month for each product. By using the LAG function and setting it to partition by ProductID, we're able to look back at the previous month's sales for each individual product. This is especially useful for tracking month-to-month changes in sales, helping you easily compare each product's performance over time.

In this query:

- **PARTITION BY ProductID** ensures that the previous month's sales are only compared within each product.
- **ORDER BY Month** arranges the sales data chronologically for each product.

This query returns the sales amount for each month, along with the previous month's sales amount in a new column called **PreviousMonthSales**. This lets you calculate month-over-month changes directly in SQL, which is useful for identifying trends or drops in sales.

Similarly, **LEAD** works the same way, but instead of looking at the previous row, it looks at the next row. For example, if you wanted to compare each month's sales to the following month's sales, you could use **LEAD(SalesAmount)**.

Practical Scenarios for Using Window Functions

Let's look at some real-world scenarios to see how these window functions are applied.

1. **Customer Retention Analysis**: Use **ROW_NUMBER** to assign a sequence to each customer's orders, helping you analyze retention by looking at repeat purchases over time.

2. **Top Performers by Department**: Use **RANK** to find the top-performing employees in each department based on sales or productivity, even when there are ties.

3. **Month-over-Month Sales Trends**: Use **LAG** to compare monthly sales for each product, identifying trends, growth, or declines over time.

4. **Customer Behavior Patterns**: Use **LEAD** to look at the next purchase date for each customer, helping you analyze the typical time between purchases.

In this section, we covered some powerful SQL window functions—**ROW_NUMBER, RANK, LEAD**, and **LAG**—and showed how they're used for statistical analysis and time-based comparisons. These functions allow you to perform complex calculations over specific sets of rows, giving you valuable insights without altering the structure of your result set.

By mastering these window functions, you'll be able to conduct sophisticated data analysis directly in SQL, making your work more efficient and insightful.

Data Cleaning and Transformation with SQL

Data Preprocessing with SQL

In this section, we'll cover methods to clean and transform raw data directly in SQL, allowing for immediate preprocessing at the database level. When working with large datasets, cleaning and transforming data at the source can save time and improve the efficiency of downstream analysis. We'll look at some commonly used SQL functions for data preprocessing, including **TRIM, CASE,** and **COALESCE.** These functions will help you clean up messy data, handle missing values, and create standardized outputs.

TRIM: Removing Extra Spaces

Let's start with **TRIM.** The TRIM function is used to remove unwanted spaces from the beginning and end of a string. Extra spaces are common in raw data and can cause issues, especially when matching or comparing values.

Imagine you have a **Customers** table with a **Name** column, but some names have extra spaces at the beginning or end. These spaces can create inconsistencies and make it difficult to search for specific names.

Here's how you would use the TRIM function to remove unwanted spaces in SQL.

```
SELECT CustomerID,
TRIM(Name) AS CleanedName
FROM Customers;
```

In this query:

- The **TRIM(Name)** function removes any leading and trailing spaces from each name in the Name column.
- Using **AS CleanedName** renames the output column to indicate that it's the cleaned version of the name.

If you only want to remove spaces from the beginning or end, SQL also offers **LTRIM** for removing spaces from the left and **RTRIM** for removing them from the right. To recap, TRIM is a simple yet powerful tool for ensuring consistent formatting by cleaning up unwanted spaces in text fields.

CASE: Creating Conditional Values

Next, let's look at the **CASE** statement. CASE is like an IF-THEN-ELSE statement in programming and is useful for creating new, conditional values based on existing data. You can use CASE to categorize data, handle exceptions, or create flag indicators.

Imagine an Orders table with an **OrderAmount** column, and you want to categorize orders into spending tiers: "Low," "Medium," and "High," based on the amount spent.

```
SELECT OrderID, OrderAmount,
CASE
WHEN OrderAmount < 50 THEN 'Low'
WHEN OrderAmount BETWEEN 50 AND 200 THEN
'Medium'
ELSE 'High'
END AS SpendingTier
FROM Orders;
```

In this query:

- **WHEN OrderAmount < 50 THEN 'Low'** assigns the category "Low" to orders with an amount less than 50.
- **WHEN OrderAmount BETWEEN 50 AND 200 THEN 'Medium'** categorizes orders between 50 and 200 as "Medium."
- **ELSE 'High'** assigns "High" to all other orders.

The CASE statement is versatile and allows you to create custom categories or classifications based on various conditions, which is especially helpful for organizing data for analysis.

COALESCE: Handling Missing Values

Now, let's talk about **COALESCE**. This function is essential for managing missing values. COALESCE returns the first non-NULL value in a list, so you can replace NULLs with default values.

Imagine a **Products** table with a **Discount** column. If some products don't have a discount value, the column shows NULL. To replace these NULLs with a default discount of 0, you'd use COALESCE.

SELECT ProductID, Price,
COALESCE(Discount, 0) AS Discount
FROM Products;

In this query:

- **COALESCE(Discount, 0)** replaces any NULL values in the Discount column with 0.
- **AS Discount** renames the output column, making it clear that this is the final discount value.

This function is particularly useful when you need to perform calculations on columns that may contain NULLs. By replacing NULLs with a default value, COALESCE ensures consistency and prevents errors in calculations.

To summarize, COALESCE helps manage missing data by providing fallback values, making your data cleaner and more reliable.

Practical Scenarios for Data Preprocessing with SQL

Let's go through a few real-world examples of how these functions can work together in data cleaning.

1. **Standardizing Customer Names:** Use TRIM to remove extra spaces, CASE to correct inconsistent capitalization or misspellings, and COALESCE to fill in missing values in optional fields like middle names.

2. **Categorizing Spending Levels:** Use CASE to create spending tiers, making it easy to segment customers or orders by their spending behavior.

3. **Handling Missing Values in Financial Data:** Use COALESCE to replace NULL values in columns

like discounts, taxes, or fees, ensuring calculations aren't disrupted by missing data.

Conclusion

In this section, we've explored essential SQL functions for data preprocessing, including **TRIM**, **CASE**, and **COALESCE**. These functions allow you to clean and transform raw data directly within the database, making it analysis-ready without needing to export it to another tool. Mastering these SQL functions enables you to handle messy data more effectively, ensuring consistency and quality in your datasets. These skills are foundational for data analysts, helping you deliver cleaner, more reliable insights.

Creating Temporary Tables and Views

Now, let's look at temporary tables and views in SQL. These structures are incredibly valuable for efficient data analysis, especially in real-time analytics. Temporary tables and views allow you to store the results of complex queries, making it easier to reuse data or build on previous calculations without rerunning the same code repeatedly. Let's start with temporary tables.

Temporary Tables: Storing Data for Short-Term Use

Temporary tables are tables created within your SQL session to store data temporarily. They're ideal for breaking down complex queries into manageable steps, making your analysis more efficient. Once your session ends or the temporary table is dropped, it's automatically deleted, so it doesn't take up permanent space in your database.

Imagine you're working with a large **Sales** table and want to calculate each customer's total spending. Instead of recalculating this every time, you can store the result in a temporary table and use it in multiple queries.

CREATE TEMPORARY TABLE CustomerSpending AS
SELECT CustomerID, SUM(TotalAmount) AS TotalSpent
FROM Sales
GROUP BY CustomerID;

In this example:

- **CREATE TEMPORARY TABLE CustomerSpending** creates a new temporary table called CustomerSpending.
- **AS** defines the data you want to store in this table—in this case, the total spending for each customer.

Once created, you can use this temporary table in other queries as if it were a regular table. For example, you could join it with a Customers table to get more information about high-spending customers.

SELECT c.CustomerID, c.Name, cs.TotalSpent
FROM Customers c
JOIN CustomerSpending cs ON c.CustomerID = cs.CustomerID
WHERE cs.TotalSpent > 500;

This query joins the **CustomerSpending** temporary table with the **Customers** table, allowing you to identify customers who have spent more than 500 quickly. Temporary tables are especially useful for organizing intermediate results in complex analyses and help reduce the need to rerun time-consuming calculations.

Views: Creating Reusable Virtual Tables

Now, let's talk about views. A view is a virtual table that's based on the result of a query. Unlike temporary tables, views don't store data physically. Instead, they store a SQL query that's executed each time the view is referenced. This makes views great for creating reusable query structures without storing actual data.

Views are especially helpful when you have complex calculations or filters that you want to apply consistently across multiple analyses.

Imagine you have a Transactions table, and you want to create a view that shows only high-value transactions—those where the total is above 1,000.

CREATE VIEW HighValueTransactions AS
SELECT TransactionID, CustomerID,
TransactionDate, TotalAmount
FROM Transactions
WHERE TotalAmount > 1000;

In this example:

- **CREATE VIEW HighValueTransactions** defines a new view called HighValueTransactions.
- The query inside the view selects only transactions where the TotalAmount is greater than 1,000.

Now, whenever you reference HighValueTransactions in a query, SQL will apply this filter automatically, saving you from having to rewrite the condition each time. For instance, you could join this view with a Customers table to retrieve names of customers who made high-value transactions:

SELECT c.Name, hvt.TotalAmount, hvt.TransactionDate
FROM Customers c
JOIN HighValueTransactions hvt ON c.CustomerID = hvt.CustomerID;

This query retrieves customer names alongside their high-value transactions, using the view to keep your SQL clean and concise.

Key Differences Between Temporary Tables and Views

To summarize the main differences:

- **Temporary Tables** physically store data for the duration of your session, making them ideal for intermediate steps in a multi-step analysis and avoiding recalculations.
- **Views** are virtual tables that don't store data but store a query instead, useful for creating reusable, simplified views of complex queries you need often.

Temporary tables and views are both powerful tools with distinct purposes: temporary tables for short-term storage and views for reusable query structures.

Practical Scenarios for Using Temporary Tables and Views

Here are a few real-world scenarios where temporary tables and views can simplify your work:

1. **Complex Data Transformation** – Use temporary tables to store intermediate results, such as calculations or aggregations, for more efficient analysis without repeating calculations.

2. **Data Filtering for Analysis** – Create views to filter data, like high-value transactions or active customers, so you can reuse these filtered datasets in multiple queries without reapplying the filter each time.

3. **Organizing Multi-Step Queries** – Use both temporary tables and views in large, multi-step analyses. Temporary tables handle intermediate data, while views simplify repeated query structures.

Conclusion

In this section, we covered temporary tables and views, which allow you to preprocess, organize, and simplify data directly in SQL. Mastering these tools gives you the ability to handle complex queries in a structured, reusable way, providing greater flexibility and control in your data analysis tasks. These skills are essential for real-time analytics, where efficient data processing is key to delivering fast, reliable insights.

Optimization Tips

In this section, we'll cover essential optimization techniques that improve the performance of your SQL queries, especially when working with large datasets. As a data analyst, efficient querying is key to managing large databases effectively. Slow queries can delay your analysis and consume unnecessary resources, so understanding optimization can make a big difference.

We'll look at three main areas: **Indexing, Query Optimization**, and **Best Practices**. By mastering these techniques, you'll be able to speed up your queries, reduce server load, and improve overall efficiency in your data analysis work.

Indexing: Making Data Retrieval Faster

Let's start with indexing. An **index** is a data structure that improves the speed of data retrieval on specific columns in a table. Think of an index like the index at the back of a book— it allows you to find information quickly without having to read every page. In SQL, indexing does the same for columns in your database tables.

For example, if you frequently search for customers by their **CustomerID** in a large **Customers** table, creating an index on **CustomerID** will make those searches much faster.

Imagine you have a Transactions table, and you want to create a view that shows only high-value transactions, specifically those where the total amount is over 1,000.

To do this, you'd write:

CREATE VIEW HighValueTransactions AS
SELECT TransactionID, CustomerID,
TransactionDate, TotalAmount
FROM Transactions
WHERE TotalAmount > 1000;

In this example:

- **CREATE VIEW HighValueTransactions** creates a new view named HighValueTransactions.
- The query inside the view filters for transactions where the **TotalAmount** is greater than 1,000.

Now, whenever you reference HighValueTransactions in a query, SQL automatically applies this filter, saving you from having to rewrite the condition each time. For instance, you could join this view with a Customers table to get the names of customers who made high-value transactions.

Key Differences Between Temporary Tables and Views

To summarize, here's a quick comparison:

- **Temporary Tables** physically store data for your session and are ideal for multi-step analyses, letting you avoid recalculating results repeatedly.
- **Views** are virtual tables that store a query, not the data itself, allowing for simplified, reusable views of complex queries.

Both tools have unique advantages: temporary tables are perfect for temporary storage, while views are great for creating reusable query structures.

Practical Scenarios for Using Temporary Tables and Views

Let's look at a few real-world examples of how temporary tables and views can make your work more efficient:

1. **Complex Data Transformation:** Use temporary tables to store intermediate results, making your analysis more efficient without rerunning calculations.

2. **Data Filtering for Analysis:** Create views to filter data, like high-value transactions, so you can reuse these filtered datasets in multiple queries.

3. **Organizing Multi-Step Queries:** Use temporary tables for intermediate steps and views for simplifying repeated query structures in large, multi-step analyses.

Conclusion

In this section, we covered the basics of temporary tables and views in SQL. These tools allow you to preprocess, organize, and simplify data, making your analysis more efficient and queries easier to manage. Mastering temporary tables and views will help you handle complex queries with structure and reusability, giving you greater flexibility in data analysis.

Building Reusable SQL Code

Stored Procedures and Functions

Now, let's move on to two powerful tools for building reusable SQL code: **stored procedures** and **functions**. These tools allow you to create repeatable workflows, saving time and reducing errors. With stored procedures and functions, you can automate tasks and standardize calculations, making your SQL code more efficient. Let's start by understanding the difference between stored procedures and functions.

Understanding Stored Procedures and Functions

Stored procedures and functions are both reusable blocks of code in SQL, but they serve slightly different purposes:

- **Stored Procedures**: Used to perform a series of SQL statements, often including conditional logic or loops. Procedures can accept parameters, making them ideal for automating complex workflows.
- **Functions**: Designed to perform calculations or return a single result. Unlike procedures, functions usually return a specific value and are commonly used within other queries.

Let's explore how to create each of these.

Creating a Stored Procedure

Imagine you work for a company that wants a monthly sales report for a specific region. Instead of running the same queries each month, you can create a stored procedure to automate the process.

```
CREATE PROCEDURE
GenerateMonthlySalesReport
@Region VARCHAR(50),
@StartDate DATE,
@EndDate DATE
AS
BEGIN
SELECT ProductID, SUM(TotalAmount) AS
MonthlySales
FROM Sales
WHERE Region = @Region
AND OrderDate BETWEEN @StartDate AND
@EndDate
GROUP BY ProductID;
END;
```

In this example:

- **CREATE PROCEDURE GenerateMonthlySalesReport** defines a new procedure.
- **@Region, @StartDate,** and **@EndDate** are parameters, allowing you to specify the region and date range.
- **AS** and **BEGIN...END** define the SQL statements within the procedure, calculating each product's total sales for a specified region and date range.

After creating this procedure, you can call it with different parameters for different regions or months.

EXEC GenerateMonthlySalesReport 'North', '2024-01-01', '2024-01-31';

This command runs the procedure for the "North" region, generating the sales report for January 2024. Stored procedures allow you to encapsulate complex logic into a single, reusable command, making workflows more efficient.

Creating a Function

Functions are generally used for calculations or transformations that you want to apply repeatedly in queries. Unlike stored procedures, functions return a single value, which can be directly used in SQL statements.

Imagine you need to apply a discount to prices in a Products table, with a frequently changing discount rate. Instead of recalculating it each time, you can create a function to apply the discount dynamically.

```
CREATE FUNCTION CalculateDiscountedPrice
(@Price DECIMAL(10, 2), @DiscountRate
DECIMAL(5, 2))
RETURNS DECIMAL(10, 2)
AS
BEGIN
RETURN @Price * (1 - @DiscountRate / 100);
END;
```

In this example:

- **CREATE FUNCTION CalculateDiscountedPrice** defines a function called CalculateDiscountedPrice.

- **@Price** and **@DiscountRate** are input parameters for the original price and discount rate.
- **RETURNS DECIMAL(10, 2)** specifies that the function returns a decimal value with two decimal places.
- **RETURN @Price * (1 - @DiscountRate / 100)** calculates the discounted price.

Once created, you can use this function in other queries to calculate discounted prices on the fly.

SELECT ProductID, Price, dbo.CalculateDiscountedPrice(Price, 10) AS DiscountedPrice FROM Products;

This query selects each product's original price and applies a 10% discount using the CalculateDiscountedPrice function. With this function, you can easily adjust the discount rate across all products without rewriting the calculation.

Query Optimization: Writing Efficient SQL Code

Now, let's talk about query optimization—writing SQL in a way that minimizes database processing. Here are some key techniques:

1. **Avoid SELECT ***: Instead of retrieving all columns with SELECT *, specify only the columns you need. This reduces data retrieval time, especially in large tables.

2. **Use WHERE Clauses to Filter Data Early**: Adding a WHERE clause to filter data as soon as possible helps the database retrieve only relevant rows, speeding up queries.

3. **Avoid Functions on Indexed Columns in WHERE Clauses**: When using a function in a WHERE clause on an indexed column, it can disable the index. Use range conditions instead to keep the index effective.

4. **Optimize JOINs by Filtering First**: Filter tables before joining, if possible, to reduce the number of rows involved in the join.

Best Practices for Performance and Efficiency

1. **Use Aliases for Readability**: Short names for tables and columns make complex queries easier to read.

2. **Monitor Query Performance**: Use database tools like Query Analyzer or Execution Plans to review performance.

3. **Limit Subqueries**: Excessive subqueries can slow performance. Replace them with JOINs or temporary tables when possible.

4. **Periodically Update Statistics**: Databases use statistics for query optimization. Keep these updated to ensure accurate performance.

5. **Archive Old Data**: Large datasets can slow queries. Consider archiving data that's no longer needed for daily operations.

Conclusion

In this chapter, we covered indexing, query optimization, stored procedures, and functions. By applying these techniques, you can significantly improve the speed and efficiency of your queries, especially with large datasets.

Optimizing SQL queries not only saves time but also reduces server load, making your data analysis more scalable.

These skills are essential for data analysts working with complex databases, helping you deliver fast, reliable insights.

End-of-Chapter Exercise: Real-World Application - Designing a Data Analytics Workflow

Imagine you're a data analyst for an online retail company aiming to monitor sales performance, track customer segments, and identify high-value products. This exercise will guide you through building a workflow that supports these goals, ensuring data quality, efficiency, and reusability.

Step 1: Data Cleaning and Transformation

Use SQL to:

1. **Remove Extra Spaces** in customer names with the TRIM function.
2. **Fill in Missing Values** in the TotalAmount column with COALESCE, replacing NULL with 0.

3. **Categorize Customers by Age Group** using the CASE statement.

Step 2: Creating Reusable Queries with Views and Temporary Tables

1. **Create a View for High-Value Orders** to filter orders with a TotalAmount over $500.
2. **Create a Temporary Table for Monthly Sales** to store monthly totals, which simplifies trend tracking.

Step 3: Generating Actionable Reports

1. **Monthly Sales Report by Product Category**: Track total monthly sales by category.
2. **Customer Segmentation Report**: Show total spending per customer by age group.
3. **Top Products Report**: Identify the top 5 products based on sales.

Step 4: Simulating a Live Analytics Environment

To handle daily updates, consider refreshing temporary tables and views regularly, and automate processes with stored procedures.

Conclusion

By completing this exercise, you've designed a complete SQL-based workflow for cleaning, organizing, and analyzing data. These skills are crucial for real-world data analysis tasks, helping you build efficient, reusable workflows and delivering insights directly from the database.

Chapter 3: Data Manipulation in Python and R for Intermediate Analysts

Exploring Data Frames for Complex Analysis

Advanced Data Frame Techniques

In this section, we'll dive into advanced techniques for working with data frames in Python and R. Data frames are the backbone of data manipulation in both languages, allowing analysts to store, organize, and transform data effectively. Here, we'll cover some intermediate-level techniques, including **multi-indexing in Pandas**, **merging large datasets**, and **handling missing data**.

These skills will help you manage and analyze complex datasets with greater precision, flexibility, and efficiency.

Multi-Indexing in Pandas (Python)

Multi-indexing allows you to use multiple levels of indexing in a data frame, making it easier to work with hierarchical or grouped data. This is especially useful when you have datasets with natural hierarchies, like sales data organized by region and product, or stock prices grouped by company and date.

Imagine you have a DataFrame called **sales_data** with columns like **Region**, **Product**, **Year**, and **Sales**. By setting up a multi-index in Python's Pandas, you can organize this data hierarchically, making it quicker to access and analyze at multiple levels.

Setting Up a Multi-Index

To create a multi-index in Pandas, you use the **set_index** function. Start by defining sample data with columns for **Region**, **Product**, **Year**, and **Sales**. Then, create a DataFrame and apply the **set_index** function with **Region** and **Product** as the index levels. This lets you access subsets of data based on these levels. For instance, to view sales data for the **North** region and **Product A**, you can specify these index levels directly.

Benefits of Multi-Indexing

Multi-indexing offers several advantages:

- It organizes data hierarchically, making it easy to perform grouped calculations.
- You can filter data efficiently by specifying levels in the index.
- It enables you to aggregate data at different levels, such as calculating total sales by region or product.

Merging Large Datasets in Python and R

Merging datasets is crucial for combining information from multiple sources. Both Python's Pandas and R's dplyr package provide efficient methods to merge large datasets.

Merging in Python (Pandas)

In Pandas, you can merge two datasets using the **merge** function. Suppose you have **customers** and **orders** DataFrames, where **customers** includes **CustomerID** and **Name**, and **orders** includes **CustomerID**, **OrderDate**, and **Amount**. Use **pd.merge** with the **on** parameter set to **CustomerID** to combine them based on matching IDs.

Specifying **how='inner'** includes only matching rows. Other join types include **left**, **right**, and **outer**.

Merging in R (dplyr)

In R, the dplyr package provides **left_join**, **right_join**, **inner_join**, and **full_join** functions for merging. Suppose **customers** and **orders** are data frames with **CustomerID** as the shared column. Using **left_join(customers, orders, by = "CustomerID")** merges the two tables on **CustomerID**, retaining all rows from **customers** and matching rows from **orders**.

Handling Missing Data in Python and R

Dealing with missing data is essential for clean analysis. Both Python and R offer flexible methods to handle missing values.

Handling Missing Data in Python (Pandas)

In Pandas, you can identify missing values with **isnull().sum()** to get a count of missing values per column. To fill missing values with the column mean, use **fillna** on the column, specifying the mean as the replacement value. To remove rows with missing values, use **dropna**.

Handling Missing Data in R (dplyr)

In R, **is.na** can identify missing values in a column, and **sum(is.na(column))** provides the count. To fill missing values with the column mean, use **mutate** with **ifelse** to conditionally replace **NA** values. To remove rows with any missing values, use **drop_na** from dplyr.

Properly managing missing data ensures the integrity of your analysis.

Conclusion

This section covers advanced data handling techniques in Python and R, including multi-indexing, merging large datasets, and managing missing data. Mastering these techniques will equip you to handle complex datasets more effectively, making your analysis structured, accurate, and efficient.

Chapter 4: Advanced Statistical Methods: Beyond the Basics

Regression Analysis for Predictive Insights

Multiple and Logistic Regression

Regression analysis is a powerful tool for predictive modeling. It allows analysts to understand relationships between variables, make predictions, and gain insights from data. In this section, we'll dive into two advanced regression techniques: **Multiple Regression** and **Logistic Regression**. Each technique will be demonstrated with case studies to show how these methods can be used for customer segmentation and risk analysis.

Multiple regression is commonly used to predict a continuous outcome based on multiple independent variables, while logistic regression is suited for binary classification problems, such as predicting whether a customer will purchase a product or default on a loan.

Multiple Regression for Customer Segmentation

Overview

Multiple regression is an extension of simple linear regression that allows you to include multiple independent variables to predict a single continuous dependent variable. This method is particularly useful for understanding the factors that influence customer behavior, such as spending, satisfaction, or likelihood to purchase.

In this example, we'll use multiple regression to predict **Customer Spending** based on multiple predictors: **Age**, **Income**, and **Number of Visits** to the store.

Example Case Study: Predicting Customer Spending

Suppose you work for a retail company that wants to identify the factors influencing customer spending. By understanding these drivers, the company can target specific customer segments more effectively.

Step 1: Prepare the Data

Assume you have a dataset with the following columns:

- **CustomerID**: Unique identifier for each customer.

- **Age**: Age of the customer.
- **Income**: Annual income of the customer.
- **Visits**: Number of visits to the store in the past year.
- **Spending**: Total spending in the store over the past year.

To start analyzing this dataset, load it into Python or R. Begin by creating a small dataset with variables like **Age**, **Income**, **Visits**, and **Spending**. This allows you to simulate customer data for practice in building a regression model.

Step 2: Building the Multiple Regression Model

In Python, you can use the **statsmodels** library to create a multiple regression model, which will help identify the relationship between multiple factors (independent variables) and customer **Spending** (dependent variable). Define the dependent variable (**Spending**) and select independent variables like **Age**, **Income**, and **Visits**. Add a constant term for the intercept and then fit the model to the data. The model's summary will include important metrics, like coefficients, R-squared values, and p-values, all of which help you understand the impact of each factor on spending behavior.

- **Age**: A positive coefficient here would suggest that older customers tend to spend more.
- **Income**: If positive, it would indicate that higher-income customers spend more.
- **Visits**: A positive coefficient for **Visits** implies that more frequent visits correlate with increased spending.

Interpreting Multiple Regression Results

By examining the coefficients, you can interpret the impact of each factor on spending. For example, if **Income** has a strong positive effect, the retail company may decide to target high-income customers. This approach allows the company to refine its strategy based on customer segments that are likely to contribute more to revenue.

Logistic Regression for Risk Analysis

Logistic regression is ideal for binary classification tasks—predicting whether an outcome will be one of two categories, such as Yes/No or 0/1. It's widely used in risk analysis scenarios, such as estimating the likelihood of a customer making a purchase. This section walks through how to use logistic regression to predict a customer's purchase behavior based on various factors.

Example: Predicting Customer Purchase Likelihood

Consider an e-commerce company aiming to forecast if a customer will make a purchase. Variables include **CustomerID** (for unique identification), **Age, Income, Previous Purchases**, and a binary **Purchase** outcome (1 for Yes, 0 for No). With this data, you can develop a logistic regression model to predict which customers are more likely to buy, helping the company optimize marketing outreach.

Step 1: Preparing the Data

Simulate this dataset by including **Age, Income, Previous Purchases**, and **Purchase** as columns in a DataFrame.

Step 2: Building the Logistic Regression Model

Using **statsmodels** in Python, set **Purchase** as the dependent variable and **Age, Income**, and **Previous Purchases** as independent variables. Fit the model and check the summary output to evaluate the relationships.

By examining the coefficients, you'll gain insights into the predictors' impact on the likelihood of purchase. A positive coefficient for **Income**, for instance, would imply that higher-income customers are more likely to make a purchase. Similarly, a positive **Previous Purchases** coefficient would indicate that customers who bought previously have a higher chance of buying again.

Summary

Multiple regression helps identify how different factors influence spending, while logistic regression estimates the likelihood of specific outcomes, such as purchases. Using these models, a company can make data-driven decisions to focus on high-value customers and optimize marketing strategies for those likely to engage.

In this example:

- **y = data['Purchase']** sets the dependent variable to Purchase.
- **X = data[['Age', 'Income', 'PreviousPurchases']]** sets the independent variables.
- **sm.Logit(y, X).fit()** fits the logistic regression model.

The output shows the coefficients and p-values, helping you understand the significance of each variable.

Step 3: Interpret the Results

The coefficients represent the effect of each predictor on the log-odds of the outcome (whether the customer will purchase or not):

- **Age**: A positive coefficient suggests that older customers are more likely to purchase.
- **Income**: A positive coefficient indicates that higher income increases purchase likelihood.
- **PreviousPurchases**: A positive coefficient means that customers with more previous purchases are more likely to buy again.

Step 4: Predict and Evaluate the Model

After building the logistic regression model, it's time to put it to the test by making predictions and evaluating its accuracy.

Start by using the model to make predictions. These predictions will be probabilities that indicate the likelihood of each outcome. To turn these probabilities into clear "yes" or "no" (or "0" and "1") results, set a threshold—for instance, considering any probability above 0.5 as a "yes."

Once predictions are made, calculate the model's accuracy by comparing the predictions to the actual outcomes. This accuracy score tells you how often the model correctly predicted the outcome, giving you a quick look at its overall reliability.

In this example:

- If the calculated accuracy is 0.80, it means the model is correctly predicting outcomes 80% of the time.

Summary: Logistic regression provides insights into which factors influence purchase likelihood. The e-commerce company can use these insights to target customers more likely to buy, improving marketing efficiency.

Practical Applications of Multiple and Logistic Regression

1. **Customer Segmentation**: Multiple regression helps in understanding factors that influence customer spending, loyalty, and satisfaction, aiding in better segmentation and targeted marketing.

2. **Risk Analysis in Finance**: Logistic regression is valuable for predicting loan defaults, credit card fraud, or insurance claims, helping financial institutions manage risk.

3. **Healthcare Analysis**: Logistic regression is often used to predict patient outcomes (e.g., survival rates, disease presence) based on multiple factors like age, blood pressure, and cholesterol levels.

4. **Employee Retention**: Multiple regression can be used to predict employee turnover by analyzing factors like salary, job satisfaction, and years of experience, helping companies address retention proactively.

Conclusion

In this section, we explored multiple regression and logistic regression, two essential tools for predictive modeling. Multiple regression allows for continuous outcome prediction based on several factors, while logistic regression enables binary classification, useful in risk analysis.

By mastering these regression techniques, you'll be able to gain predictive insights from your data, making informed decisions based on statistical analysis. Whether in customer segmentation, financial risk, or healthcare analysis, regression models are powerful tools for understanding complex relationships and predicting outcomes in real-world scenarios.

Interpreting Results in Real-World Contexts

When conducting regression analysis, interpreting the results is crucial to extracting meaningful insights that can inform real-world decisions. This section will explain how to understand the main components of a regression output—**coefficients**, **p-values**, and **R-squared values**—and what they imply in practical terms.

By learning to interpret these elements, you'll be able to draw actionable conclusions from your data, making your analysis more impactful and relevant.

Understanding Coefficients

What Are Coefficients?

In regression analysis, coefficients represent the relationship between each independent variable and the dependent variable. They tell you how much the dependent variable is expected to change when the independent variable changes by one unit, assuming all other variables are held constant.

- **Positive Coefficient**: If the coefficient is positive, the dependent variable increases as the independent variable increases.
- **Negative Coefficient**: If the coefficient is negative, the dependent variable decreases as the independent variable increases.

Interpreting Coefficients in Real-World Contexts

Example 1: Customer Spending

Suppose you're analyzing the impact of **Income** and **Age** on **Customer Spending** using multiple regression. Here's an example of what the output might look like:

Variable Coefficient

Income   0.02

Age   5.00

- **Income Coefficient (0.02)**: For every additional dollar in income, customer spending is expected to increase by $0.02, assuming age remains constant.
- **Age Coefficient (5.00)**: For each additional year in age, customer spending is expected to increase by $5, assuming income remains constant.

In practical terms, this suggests that both income and age positively influence spending, but age has a stronger impact. This insight might guide the company to focus on targeting older, higher-income customers for premium products or services.

Example 2: Predicting Loan Default

In a logistic regression model predicting **Loan Default** (yes/no), you might have coefficients for **Income** and **Debt-to-Income Ratio**.

Variable	Coefficient
Income	-0.03
Debt-to-Income Ratio	0.15

- **Income Coefficient (-0.03)**: A negative coefficient for income implies that higher income reduces the likelihood of loan default.
- **Debt-to-Income Ratio Coefficient (0.15)**: A positive coefficient for debt-to-income ratio indicates that higher ratios increase the probability of default.

In real-world terms, the bank might use this information to prioritize loan applicants with lower debt-to-income ratios and higher incomes, thereby reducing the risk of default.

Note: In logistic regression, coefficients represent the change in log-odds rather than direct change in the dependent variable. However, the direction and relative size of coefficients still provide insights into how each factor influences the outcome.

Understanding p-values

What Are p-values?

A p-value is a measure of statistical significance. It tells you whether the observed relationship between the independent variable and the dependent variable is likely to be real or just due to random chance.

- **Low p-value (< 0.05)**: A p-value below 0.05 typically indicates that the variable is statistically significant, meaning there's strong evidence to suggest a real relationship between the variable and the outcome.
- **High p-value (> 0.05)**: A high p-value suggests that the variable may not have a meaningful effect on the outcome.

Interpreting p-values in Real-World Contexts

Example: Evaluating Predictors for Customer Retention

Suppose you're analyzing factors that affect **Customer Retention** and find the following results:

Variable	Coefficient	p-value
Age	4.0	0.01
Annual Income	1.5	0.06
Engagement Rate	10.0	0.0005

- **Age (p-value = 0.01)**: Since the p-value is below 0.05, age is statistically significant, suggesting it has a real impact on customer retention.
- **Annual Income (p-value = 0.06)**: This p-value is slightly above 0.05, indicating that income might not significantly impact retention in this sample. However, if income is critical to your analysis, you might consider including it in further analysis with additional data.
- **Engagement Rate (p-value = 0.0005)**: The low p-value indicates that engagement rate is highly significant, suggesting a strong relationship with customer retention.

Real-World Takeaway: This analysis shows that engagement rate has the strongest impact on customer retention, followed by age. The company may choose to focus on increasing engagement to improve retention.

Example: Risk Analysis for Credit Score

In a logistic regression model to predict **Credit Score Risk** (low/high), you might find the following p-values:

Variable	Coefficient	p-value
Income	0.05	0.001
Debt-to-Income Ratio	0.20	0.02
Marital Status	-0.10	0.08

- **Income and Debt-to-Income Ratio** have p-values below 0.05, making them statistically significant predictors of credit risk.
- **Marital Status** has a p-value of 0.08, indicating it's not statistically significant and may not be a reliable predictor in this model.

Real-World Takeaway: Focusing on income and debt-to-income ratio may be more useful for predicting credit risk, while marital status can potentially be excluded from the model to simplify it without losing predictive accuracy.

Understanding R-squared Values

What is R-squared?

R-squared (R^2) is a measure of how well the independent variables explain the variability in the dependent variable. It ranges from 0 to 1, where:

- **Higher R-squared values** (closer to 1) indicate that a large proportion of the variability in the dependent variable is explained by the model.
- **Lower R-squared values** (closer to 0) suggest that the model does not explain much of the variability, and other factors might be influencing the dependent variable.

Note: R-squared is typically used with multiple regression (not logistic regression), as logistic regression uses other measures (e.g., pseudo-R-squared).

Interpreting R-squared in Real-World Contexts

Example: Sales Prediction Model

Suppose you create a multiple regression model to predict **Monthly Sales** based on factors like **Marketing Spend**, **Store Location**, and **Season**. Your model outputs an R-squared value of 0.85.

- **R-squared = 0.85**: This means that 85% of the variability in monthly sales is explained by the independent variables in the model. This high R-squared value suggests that the model is well-suited for predicting sales based on the input factors.

Real-World Takeaway: With a high R-squared, you can confidently use this model to make sales predictions and even identify key factors, like marketing spend, that could be optimized to boost sales.

Example: Employee Satisfaction Analysis

If you create a model to predict **Employee Satisfaction** based on variables like **Salary**, **Work Hours**, and **Manager Rating** and find an R-squared value of 0.40, this suggests that only 40% of the variability in satisfaction is explained by these factors.

Real-World Takeaway: In this case, the low R-squared indicates that other variables might be influencing employee satisfaction, such as work-life balance, benefits, or career development opportunities. This insight could encourage HR to gather additional data to improve the model.

Conclusion

Interpreting regression results is crucial for drawing actionable insights from your data. By understanding coefficients, p-values, and R-squared values, you can determine the importance and impact of each variable on the outcome in real-world terms. Whether you're predicting customer behavior, assessing risk, or analyzing sales performance, interpreting these measures helps ensure that your findings are relevant, reliable, and actionable.

Mastering the interpretation of regression outputs will empower you to make data-driven decisions and communicate your findings effectively to stakeholders in business, finance, healthcare, and beyond.

Clustering and Segmentation Techniques

K-Means and Hierarchical Clustering

Clustering is a powerful technique for identifying patterns and natural groupings in data. It's particularly useful for customer segmentation, where you want to group customers based on similar characteristics, behaviors, or preferences. In this section, we'll explore two popular clustering methods: **K-Means Clustering** and **Hierarchical Clustering**.

K-Means is known for its speed and efficiency in handling large datasets, while Hierarchical Clustering provides a more flexible approach to grouping data and visualizing relationships between clusters. Both techniques offer unique insights and can be applied in various domains, such as marketing, customer segmentation, and product categorization.

K-Means Clustering

Overview

K-Means is a partitional clustering algorithm that divides the dataset into a specified number of clusters, or **K** clusters. Each data point is assigned to the nearest cluster based on the Euclidean distance to the cluster's center (called the centroid). The goal is to minimize the distance between data points and their cluster centroids, making each cluster as cohesive as possible.

K-Means is widely used for its simplicity and speed, making it suitable for large datasets. However, it requires the number of clusters (K) to be specified in advance.

Steps of K-Means Clustering

1. **Choose the number of clusters (K)**.
2. **Initialize cluster centroids randomly**.
3. **Assign each data point to the nearest centroid**.
4. **Update centroids** based on the mean of the assigned points.
5. **Repeat** steps 3 and 4 until the centroids no longer change significantly or a maximum number of iterations is reached.

Example Case Study: Customer Segmentation with K-Means

Suppose you work for a retail company and want to segment your customers based on their annual spending and number of store visits. Segmenting customers can help target marketing campaigns and identify high-value customers.

Step 1: Prepare the Data

Assume you have a dataset with the following columns:

- **CustomerID**: Unique identifier for each customer.
- **Annual_Spending**: Amount spent by the customer in the past year.
- **Visits**: Number of visits to the store in the past year.

Here's how you can approach customer segmentation using Python and K-Means clustering:

Step 1: Load and Prepare the Data

Start by loading the data. In this example, we have customer data with CustomerID, Annual_Spending, and Visits. We'll drop CustomerID since it's not relevant for clustering, focusing instead on Annual_Spending and Visits.

Step 2: Determine the Optimal Number of Clusters

To decide on the best number of clusters (K), use the elbow method. This method involves running K-Means for a range of cluster numbers and plotting each cluster's sum of squared distances. When plotted, the optimal K appears as an "elbow" where adding more clusters results in diminishing improvements.

Step 3: Apply K-Means Clustering

Once you have chosen the ideal number of clusters (suppose K=3), fit the K-Means model to the data. This will assign each data point (customer) to one of the clusters based on their spending and visit patterns.

Step 4: Interpret and Visualize the Clusters

Finally, visualize the clusters. Plot Annual_Spending against Visits, with each point colored by its cluster. This will help you see distinct customer segments based on their spending and visit frequency.

Each cluster represents a distinct customer segment. For example:

- **Cluster 0**: Low spenders with few visits.
- **Cluster 1**: Moderate spenders with moderate visits.
- **Cluster 2**: High spenders with frequent visits.

These insights allow the company to tailor its marketing strategy to each customer segment.

Hierarchical Clustering

Overview

Hierarchical clustering creates a tree-like structure (dendrogram) that shows how data points are grouped at various levels. It does not require specifying the number of clusters beforehand, making it useful for exploratory analysis.

There are two types of hierarchical clustering:

- **Agglomerative**: Starts with each data point as a separate cluster and merges them based on their similarity.
- **Divisive**: Starts with all data points in one cluster and splits them based on their dissimilarity.

Agglomerative clustering is more common and will be the focus here.

Steps of Hierarchical Clustering (Agglomerative)

1. **Calculate the distance** between every pair of data points.
2. **Merge the two closest clusters** to form a new cluster.
3. **Recalculate distances** between the new cluster and all other clusters.
4. **Repeat** steps 2 and 3 until only one cluster remains.

Example Case Study: Customer Segmentation with Hierarchical Clustering

Here's how you can use hierarchical clustering for customer segmentation, starting from the same customer data used in the K-Means example:

Step 1: Prepare the Data

Using the previously prepared data on customer spending and visits, select these features for clustering.

Step 2: Generate a Dendrogram

The dendrogram is a tree-like diagram that visually represents hierarchical clustering. It shows at which points data points merge into clusters and helps determine the optimal number of clusters by observing where to "cut" the tree. Using Python's scipy library, perform hierarchical clustering and calculate the dendrogram to see how clusters form at various levels.

Step 3: Apply Hierarchical Clustering

Once you have analyzed the dendrogram, you can decide on the number of clusters, for instance, three clusters. Use

AgglomerativeClustering from scikit-learn to assign each customer to a cluster based on the hierarchical structure.

Step 4: Visualize and Interpret the Clusters

Finally, plot the clusters to interpret the results, similar to the K-Means method. Each cluster will represent a distinct customer segment based on spending and visit frequency. Hierarchical clustering offers a more visual approach to clustering, with the dendrogram providing a detailed view of how clusters group together at various levels.

Choosing Between K-Means and Hierarchical Clustering

- **K-Means Clustering**: Best for large datasets with well-defined clusters. It's computationally efficient and produces distinct clusters, making it suitable for applications where you know the number of clusters in advance.
- **Hierarchical Clustering**: Ideal for smaller datasets or when you're exploring the data and unsure of the optimal number of clusters. The dendrogram helps

you understand data structure and identify the natural groupings.

Real-World Applications of Clustering Techniques

1. **Customer Segmentation**: Group customers based on demographics, purchasing behavior, or engagement metrics to tailor marketing strategies for each segment.

2. **Product Categorization**: Identify similar products based on features, enabling e-commerce platforms to recommend similar items or group products in categories.

3. **Document Clustering**: Organize documents based on topics or content similarity, useful for organizing large datasets of text or for content recommendation.

4. **Anomaly Detection**: Spot outliers in datasets by identifying items that don't belong to any cluster, useful in fraud detection and quality control.

Conclusion

In this section, we covered two popular clustering methods: **K-Means** and **Hierarchical Clustering**. Both methods allow you to group data into meaningful clusters, revealing patterns and segments that aren't immediately visible in raw data.

K-Means is well-suited for large datasets where you know the number of clusters, while Hierarchical Clustering provides flexibility in exploring data structure without needing to predefine the number of clusters. By mastering these techniques, you'll be able to apply clustering for customer segmentation, product categorization, and other applications, gaining valuable insights that can drive business decisions and improve data-driven strategies.

Evaluating Cluster Quality

After performing clustering analysis, it's essential to evaluate the quality of the clusters to ensure that the results are meaningful and useful. A good clustering solution should have well-separated clusters with cohesive points. In this section, we'll discuss key methods for assessing cluster validity, including the **silhouette score, elbow method, Dunn index**, and **Davies-Bouldin index**.

By using these evaluation metrics, you can make informed decisions about the optimal number of clusters and the overall quality of your segmentation.

Silhouette Score

Overview

The silhouette score is a popular metric for evaluating clustering quality. It measures how similar each data point is to its assigned cluster compared to other clusters. The score ranges from -1 to 1, with:

- **Values close to 1** indicating that points are well-clustered and far from other clusters.
- **Values around 0** suggesting that points are on or near the boundary between clusters.
- **Negative values** indicating that points may have been assigned to the wrong cluster.

Here's an overview of using clustering metrics like the silhouette score, elbow method, and Dunn index to evaluate and interpret clustering solutions effectively:

Silhouette Score: Understanding Cluster Quality

The silhouette score measures how distinct each cluster is, helping determine the quality of clustering by evaluating how similar each point is to its own cluster versus others. This score is calculated for each data point and ranges between -1 and 1, where higher values indicate well-defined clusters, and lower values suggest that clusters might be overlapping.

To calculate the silhouette score:

1. Run K-Means clustering with different values of KKK (the number of clusters).
2. For each KKK, calculate the score and examine which value yields the highest score, indicating the best separation between clusters.

Each data point's score is based on:

- **Intra-cluster distance** (how close the point is to others within its cluster).
- **Inter-cluster distance** (the distance to points in the nearest neighboring cluster).

If you find the silhouette score drops when increasing KKK, it could suggest "over-clustering," where the data is split too finely into multiple clusters, losing meaningful structure.

Elbow Method: Finding the Ideal Number of Clusters

The elbow method is a visual technique to determine the optimal number of clusters by examining the sum of squared distances, or **inertia**, between data points and their assigned cluster centroids. It involves plotting the inertia for various values of KKK and finding the "elbow," or point of diminishing returns, which indicates the best KKK for clustering.

To use the elbow method:

1. Run K-Means clustering with different values of KKK, typically ranging from 1 to 10.
2. Plot the inertia for each value of KKK to observe the curve.
3. Identify the "elbow" point where adding more clusters no longer significantly reduces inertia.

The point at which the curve begins to flatten is considered the ideal number of clusters, as further increases in K add little value in minimizing distances within clusters.

Dunn Index: Assessing Cluster Separation and Compactness

The Dunn index is a metric used to evaluate clustering quality by comparing the **minimum inter-cluster distance** (distance between clusters) with the **maximum intra-cluster distance** (distance within a cluster). A higher Dunn index suggests well-separated, compact clusters. This metric is especially valuable when comparing different clustering algorithms or setups, as it emphasizes both separation and cohesion of clusters.

The Dunn index calculation involves:

1. Finding the smallest distance between any two clusters.
2. Finding the largest distance within a single cluster.

This ratio yields a value indicating clustering quality—higher values mean clusters are distinct and tightly grouped.

However, keep in mind that the Dunn index can be sensitive to noise, so it's generally more effective with clearly distinct clusters.

Davies-Bouldin Index: Evaluating Cluster Quality

The Davies-Bouldin index is a measure used to assess clustering quality by calculating how similar each cluster is to its most similar neighboring cluster. In contrast to some other metrics, a **lower Davies-Bouldin index** indicates better clustering, as it suggests that clusters are more distinct and well-separated.

The formula for the Davies-Bouldin index is:

The formula for the Davies-Bouldin index is:

$$DB = \frac{1}{K} \sum_{i=1}^{K} \max_{j \neq i} \left(\frac{\sigma_i + \sigma_j}{d(c_i, c_j)} \right)$$

where:

- **KKK** is the number of clusters.

- **σi\sigma_iσi** is the average distance of points within cluster iii to its centroid.
- **d(ci,cj)d(c_i, c_j)d(ci,cj)** is the distance between the centroids of clusters iii and jjj.

In this formula, the index evaluates how compact and well-separated each cluster is from others. A lower value indicates that clusters are more compact and well-distanced from each other.

Using the Davies-Bouldin Index to Evaluate Clusters

To calculate the Davies-Bouldin index in Python, you can use the davies_bouldin_score function from the sklearn.metrics module. This is particularly useful for comparing the quality of different clustering solutions:

1. Apply clustering to your data with your chosen number of clusters, KKK.
2. Calculate the Davies-Bouldin index for the resulting cluster labels.
3. A lower score suggests better clustering performance.

For example, you can run K-Means clustering on a dataset with $K=3$ clusters and calculate the Davies-Bouldin index for the resulting clusters to evaluate how well-separated and compact the clusters are. The lower the index, the better the clustering outcome.

Interpretation: A lower Davies-Bouldin index indicates that clusters are well-separated and have minimal overlap. This metric is useful when comparing clustering solutions to find the one with the least similarity between clusters.

Choosing the Right Evaluation Metric

Each clustering metric has its strengths and weaknesses, and the choice of metric depends on the specific clustering task and dataset:

- **Silhouette Score** is ideal for quick evaluations and works well with K-Means, especially when clusters are well-defined.
- **Elbow Method** is a simple and effective way to choose the initial number of clusters for K-Means.

- **Dunn Index** is useful when you're seeking a strong separation between clusters, though it can be sensitive to noise.
- **Davies-Bouldin Index** provides a more robust assessment of cluster separation and works well when comparing different clustering algorithms.

Using a combination of these metrics often provides the best insight into cluster quality, helping you make informed decisions about clustering parameters and validation.

Conclusion

Evaluating the quality of clusters is a critical step in clustering analysis. By understanding and applying metrics like the silhouette score, elbow method, Dunn index, and Davies-Bouldin index, you can assess the validity and cohesiveness of clusters in your data. These metrics allow you to refine your clustering model, ensuring that it captures meaningful patterns and segmentation.

Mastering cluster evaluation techniques will help you create reliable and actionable clustering models, whether you're segmenting customers, categorizing products, or identifying patterns in complex datasets.

Time Series Analysis for Trend Prediction

Understanding and Forecasting Trends

Time series analysis is a powerful tool for identifying patterns and predicting future values in data collected over time. It's commonly used in fields like finance, economics, sales forecasting, and supply chain management. This section introduces two popular time series forecasting techniques—**ARIMA** (Auto-Regressive Integrated Moving Average) and **Exponential Smoothing**—and explains how to use them to forecast trends and make data-driven predictions.

By the end of this section, you'll understand the fundamentals of these techniques, how to apply them, and their applications in real-world scenarios.

Time Series Fundamentals

Before diving into forecasting methods, let's review some basic concepts in time series analysis:

- **Trend**: The long-term upward or downward movement in a time series.
- **Seasonality**: Regular patterns that repeat over specific time intervals, such as daily, weekly, or yearly.
- **Noise**: Random fluctuations or irregularities in the data that do not follow a pattern.
- **Stationarity**: A time series is stationary if its statistical properties (mean, variance) are constant over time.

Most forecasting methods aim to model the trend and seasonality while accounting for noise to make accurate predictions.

ARIMA (Auto-Regressive Integrated Moving Average)

Overview

ARIMA is one of the most widely used models for time series forecasting. It combines three components:

1. **Auto-Regressive (AR)**: A model that uses past values to predict future values.
2. **Integrated (I)**: A differencing step to make the time series stationary, removing trends and seasonality.
3. **Moving Average (MA)**: A model that uses past forecast errors to improve predictions.

ARIMA models are defined by three parameters: **(p, d, q)**:

- **p**: The number of lag observations in the auto-regression model.
- **d**: The number of times differencing is applied to make the series stationary.
- **q**: The size of the moving average window.

Steps for Applying ARIMA

1. **Make the Series Stationary**: Use differencing if needed to remove trends or seasonality.
2. **Identify Optimal Parameters (p, d, q)**: Use methods like **autocorrelation** and **partial autocorrelation** plots, or try different combinations to find the best fit.

3. **Fit the Model**: Train the ARIMA model on your data.

4. **Forecast**: Use the model to make predictions and evaluate its performance.

Example: Sales Forecasting with ARIMA

Suppose you want to forecast monthly sales for the upcoming year based on historical sales data. Here's how you can use ARIMA to achieve this in Python.

Step-by-Step Guide for Time Series Forecasting with ARIMA and Exponential Smoothing

Step 1: Load and Visualize the Data

First, start by loading your dataset and visualizing it to get an initial sense of the data's trend and pattern over time. For example, if you're analyzing monthly sales data, you can use a line chart to see the fluctuations and any potential seasonality.

Step 2: Make the Series Stationary

Time series forecasting models like ARIMA work best when the data is stationary, meaning it has a consistent mean and variance over time. To achieve this, apply differencing if you detect a trend. Differencing essentially subtracts the previous data point from the current one, helping to stabilize the trend.

Step 3: Determine ARIMA Parameters

To configure an ARIMA model, you need three parameters:

- **p**: The number of lag observations included.
- **d**: The degree of differencing needed to make the series stationary.
- **q**: The size of the moving average window.

Using autocorrelation (ACF) and partial autocorrelation (PACF) plots helps to identify these values visually, but an automated tool like auto_arima can suggest optimal parameters for you, simplifying the setup.

Step 4: Fit the Model and Forecast

After identifying the best parameters, fit the ARIMA model. Then, use it to forecast future values. If, for example, you want a 12-month forecast, set your forecast steps to 12. Plotting both historical and forecasted values can visually validate the model's performance.

Applications

ARIMA is ideal for non-seasonal data with trends, widely used in economic and financial forecasting, sales predictions, and demand planning.

Exponential Smoothing: An Alternative Approach for Trend and Seasonality

Overview

Exponential Smoothing models are useful for time series with different components, such as level, trend, and seasonality. There are three main types:

1. **Simple Exponential Smoothing (SES)**: For data without trend or seasonality.

2. **Holt's Linear Trend Model**: For data with a trend but no seasonality.

3. **Holt-Winters Seasonal Model**: For data with both trend and seasonality.

Each type uses smoothing parameters to control the weight given to recent data points:

- **Alpha (α)**: Controls smoothing of the level.
- **Beta (β)**: Controls smoothing of the trend.
- **Gamma (γ)**: Controls smoothing of the seasonality.

Example: Forecasting Seasonal Sales with Holt-Winters

Suppose you're dealing with seasonal sales data and want to apply the Holt-Winters model. Here's how to proceed:

1. **Fit the Holt-Winters Model**: Using ExponentialSmoothing from Python's statsmodels library, you can specify both trend and seasonality as additive components if the pattern is additive.

2. **Set Seasonality Parameters**: For monthly data with annual seasonality, specify seasonal_periods=12.

3. **Visualize the Forecast**: As with ARIMA, visualize both the historical and forecasted data to evaluate the model's predictions.

Applications

Exponential Smoothing is ideal for data with seasonality and trends, making it useful for industries like retail, where sales and demand often follow seasonal patterns. It's also beneficial in inventory management and any scenario involving periodic time series data.

Choosing Between ARIMA and Exponential Smoothing

- **ARIMA** is suitable for time series with a trend and no seasonality, particularly when the data is stationary or can be made stationary through differencing.
- **Exponential Smoothing** (especially Holt-Winters) is ideal for data with trend and seasonality. It's often easier to interpret and implement, especially for seasonally varying data.

Practical Applications of Time Series Forecasting

1. **Sales Forecasting**: Predict monthly or quarterly sales based on historical patterns, helping companies optimize inventory and resource planning.

2. **Demand Planning**: Use forecasts to anticipate demand, reducing overstock and stockouts, which is crucial in retail, manufacturing, and supply chain management.

3. **Economic Forecasting**: Project future economic indicators, such as GDP or inflation, to inform government policy or business strategy.

4. **Financial Market Analysis**: Forecast stock prices or trading volumes, helping investors and analysts make informed decisions.

5. **Utility and Resource Forecasting**: Predict energy consumption or water demand based on past usage patterns, assisting utility companies in planning resource allocation.

Conclusion

In this section, we introduced time series forecasting techniques—**ARIMA** and **Exponential Smoothing**—which are essential tools for predicting trends in temporal data. Both methods offer unique advantages, with ARIMA suitable for stationary data with trends and Exponential Smoothing well-suited for seasonal data with trends.

By mastering these techniques, you can develop robust forecasting models for applications ranging from sales and demand forecasting to economic and financial analysis. Time series forecasting is a valuable skill that enables data analysts to extract actionable insights from historical data, empowering data-driven decision-making in various industries.

Case Study in Forecasting: Sales Prediction

Time series forecasting is widely used in business applications to predict future values based on historical data. In this case study, we'll walk through a real-world example of **sales forecasting** for a retail company. Using historical monthly sales data, we'll apply time series techniques—**ARIMA** and **Holt-Winters Exponential Smoothing**—to generate a forecast that can help the company anticipate future sales and make informed business decisions.

By following this case study, you'll gain a deeper understanding of how to apply these forecasting methods and interpret the results in a business context.

Business Scenario

Imagine a retail company that sells seasonal products. The company wants to forecast monthly sales for the next year to plan inventory, allocate resources, and optimize marketing strategies. They have collected monthly sales data for the past five years and want to use this historical data to predict sales trends.

Data Overview

The dataset contains:

- **Date**: The month and year for each data point.
- **Sales**: The total sales for each month (in dollars).

The goal is to analyze the time series data to understand the trend and seasonality, and then generate a forecast for the next 12 months.

Step 1: Data Exploration and Visualization

Start by loading the sales data and visualizing it to identify any overall trends, seasonal patterns, or recurring peaks. This step is essential to understand the general behavior of sales over time, which will guide the choice of forecasting method.

1. Load the data and plot the time series to observe monthly sales trends.
2. Look for key patterns, such as whether sales show a steady increase (upward trend) or if they peak seasonally, for example, during holiday periods.

In our example, let's assume that sales data shows a clear upward trend with predictable peaks around certain months, such as the holiday season.

Step 2: Applying ARIMA for Forecasting

ARIMA (AutoRegressive Integrated Moving Average) is effective for data with trends but limited seasonality.

Step 2.1: Make the Series Stationary

ARIMA models require the data to be stationary, meaning it has a constant mean and variance over time. Applying "differencing" helps remove trends and stabilize the data.

1. Perform differencing on the dataset to remove the trend.
2. Visualize the differenced data to confirm it is now stationary, showing less trend over time.

Step 2.2: Identify Optimal ARIMA Parameters

To configure ARIMA, three parameters are needed: **p** (auto-regression), **d** (degree of differencing), and **q** (moving average).

- Use the auto_arima function to automatically identify the best combination of these parameters.

Assume the model identifies the optimal configuration as ARIMA(1, 1, 1).

Step 2.3: Fit the ARIMA Model and Forecast

Using the identified parameters, fit the ARIMA model to the data and forecast future sales.

1. Fit the model with the chosen parameters.
2. Forecast the next 12 months to get an estimate of future sales trends.
3. Plot the historical sales alongside the forecasted values to visualize the predictions.

The ARIMA forecast projects sales based on past patterns, which is suitable if the data has a significant trend but limited seasonality.

Step 3: Applying Holt-Winters Exponential Smoothing

When the data exhibits both a trend and seasonality, the Holt-Winters (Exponential Smoothing) method is more appropriate. This approach accommodates patterns like seasonal peaks and trends over time, making it ideal for retail sales data.

Step 3.1: Fit the Holt-Winters Model

Using ExponentialSmoothing from the statsmodels library, fit the Holt-Winters model by setting both trend and seasonality as additive components, which is appropriate when these effects are consistent over time.

1. Fit the Holt-Winters model to the data, specifying both trend and seasonality settings.
2. Forecast the next 12 months.
3. Plot the historical data alongside the forecasted data to see how the model captures seasonal peaks and trends.

The Holt-Winters forecast accounts for both trend and seasonal variations, making it a strong option when you have data with regular, repeating seasonal patterns, such as holiday sales spikes.

Interpretation of Forecasts

- **ARIMA Forecast**: Suited for data with a clear trend but without strong seasonal fluctuations. It's useful for projecting future values in a straightforward trend scenario.
- **Holt-Winters Forecast**: Better for data with both trend and seasonal patterns, providing more precise

predictions for cases where seasonal spikes are expected, such as during holidays.

Using these two approaches allows you to tailor forecasting based on the presence of trends and seasonality in your data, helping to create accurate, actionable sales projections.

Step 4: Comparing Forecast Results

By applying both ARIMA and Holt-Winters models, we can compare the forecasts and choose the one that best fits the historical data. In a business setting, it's essential to choose the model that captures the trend and seasonality accurately for optimal forecasting.

Comparison Points:

- **ARIMA**: Good for capturing trends but may miss seasonal peaks if they are irregular or vary in intensity.
- **Holt-Winters**: Ideal for data with consistent seasonal patterns, as it directly incorporates seasonality into the forecast.

In practice, plot both forecasts and compare them visually and quantitatively (using metrics like **Mean Absolute Error** or **Root Mean Square Error**) to determine the best fit.

Step 5: Business Insights and Applications

With a reliable forecast, the retail company can leverage these predictions to make informed business decisions:

1. **Inventory Management**: By anticipating sales peaks, the company can stock up on products ahead of high-demand periods, reducing the risk of stockouts.
2. **Resource Allocation**: Knowing future sales trends helps the company allocate resources such as staffing, marketing budgets, and distribution efforts more effectively.
3. **Promotional Planning**: Forecasting sales allows the marketing team to plan promotions around anticipated dips, boosting sales during slow periods.
4. **Financial Planning**: Accurate sales predictions contribute to budgeting and financial forecasting,

helping the company set realistic revenue targets and optimize cash flow.

For example, if the forecast indicates a sales peak during December, the company could ramp up holiday promotions in advance, adjust staffing levels, and increase product inventory to meet demand.

Conclusion

This case study demonstrates how to apply time series analysis to a practical business problem—forecasting monthly sales. By leveraging **ARIMA** and **Holt-Winters Exponential Smoothing**, the retail company can predict future sales trends and make data-driven decisions.

Mastering time series forecasting techniques enables data analysts to generate valuable insights in various domains, including finance, retail, and supply chain management. With accurate forecasts, businesses can optimize operations, improve customer satisfaction, and ultimately enhance profitability.

End-of-Chapter Data Project: Full Predictive Analytics Workflow

In this project, you'll apply your knowledge of regression, clustering, and forecasting to complete a full predictive analytics workflow. By using SQL, Python, and R, you'll gain practical experience in integrating multiple tools and techniques, mirroring the workflows used by data analysts and scientists in real-world projects.

This project will cover:

1. Data Extraction using SQL
2. Data Preprocessing and Regression Analysis using Python
3. Clustering and Segmentation using Python
4. Forecasting using R

Dataset Overview

For this project, imagine you're working for a retail company that wants to analyze and forecast customer purchasing behavior. You have access to a dataset containing transaction data with the following columns:

- **CustomerID**: Unique identifier for each customer.
- **Age**: Age of the customer.
- **Income**: Annual income of the customer.
- **Visits**: Number of store visits in the past year.
- **Spending**: Total spending by the customer in the past year.
- **OrderDate**: Date of each purchase made by the customer.

The dataset provides insights into customer demographics, purchasing behavior, and time-based purchase patterns.

Step 1: Data Extraction using SQL

Start by retrieving the data from a SQL database. Suppose the data is stored in two tables:

- **Customers**: Contains demographic information like CustomerID, Age, and Income.
- **Transactions**: Contains transaction details, including CustomerID, OrderDate, Visits, and Spending.

Step 1: SQL Query to Retrieve Customer Data

To start, retrieve the data for customers who made at least one purchase in the past year, including their demographics and transaction details.

In SQL, the query combines customer demographic data with their transaction history over the last year:

1. **Customer and Transaction Join**: This pulls in details for each customer and transaction.
2. **Filter by Date**: Only transactions from the past year are included.

Once retrieved, save this data as a CSV file to analyze in Python or R.

Step 2: Data Preprocessing and Regression Analysis in Python

Now, load the data in Python for preprocessing and perform regression analysis to understand which factors influence customer spending.

Step 2.1: Load and Explore the Data

Load the saved CSV file and preview the first few rows to get an initial look at the data's structure.

Step 2.2: Data Cleaning

Check for missing values, especially in key columns like income. Fill missing income values with the median, and convert any date fields to a date format.

Step 2.3: Regression Analysis

Using multiple regression, analyze how factors like age, income, and visits impact customer spending. Set spending as the dependent variable and age, income, and visits as the independent variables. After running the regression, review the model's coefficients and p-values to identify significant predictors of spending.

For instance, a strong positive coefficient for income would indicate that higher-income customers tend to spend more.

Step 3: Customer Segmentation with Clustering in Python

To understand different customer behaviors, segment customers based on demographics and spending habits using clustering.

Step 3.1: Prepare Data for Clustering

For clustering, select features like age, income, visits, and spending. Normalize these features so they have equal influence during clustering.

Step 3.2: K-Means Clustering

Using K-Means, find the optimal number of clusters with the Elbow Method, which involves plotting the sum of squared distances for different values of K. Suppose the Elbow Method indicates that three clusters are optimal.

Fit the K-Means model with three clusters and label each customer according to their cluster. These clusters represent distinct customer segments. For example, one cluster might represent high-income, high-spending customers, while another could represent low-income, low-spending ones. This segmentation can help in designing targeted marketing strategies.

Step 4: Forecasting Monthly Sales in R

Switch to R to forecast monthly sales for the next year, using the Holt-Winters Exponential Smoothing method to capture both trend and seasonality.

Step 4.1: Aggregate Monthly Sales Data in Python

Before moving to R, aggregate sales by month to create a time series dataset suitable for forecasting. Save the monthly data as a CSV file for use in R.

Step 4.2: Forecasting in R with Holt-Winters

In R:

1. Load the monthly sales data and convert it to a time series format.
2. Apply the Holt-Winters Exponential Smoothing model, which accounts for trend and seasonality.
3. Forecast the next 12 months and plot the results, providing a visual representation of the expected monthly sales.

This approach helps predict future sales, making it easier to plan inventory and marketing efforts around expected seasonal trends.

Interpretation: The forecast provides expected monthly sales for the next year. This insight helps the retail company in planning inventory, budgeting, and optimizing marketing efforts for anticipated high-demand periods.

Project Summary

This project covers a complete predictive analytics workflow using SQL, Python, and R:

1. **Data Extraction**: Retrieve data from SQL and export it for analysis.
2. **Regression Analysis**: Use Python to analyze factors that influence spending.
3. **Clustering**: Segment customers into distinct groups based on behavior and demographics.
4. **Forecasting**: Use R to predict future sales based on historical patterns.

This end-to-end project showcases a multi-tool, multi-technique approach to predictive analytics, equipping you with practical skills for real-world data projects. By mastering this workflow, you'll be prepared to tackle complex data challenges and provide actionable insights across various business domains.

Chapter 5: Integrated Project: Building a Data Analytics Pipeline

Defining the Project Scope

End-to-End Analysis

Building a robust data analytics pipeline starts with a clear understanding of the project's objectives, data requirements, and analytical goals. Defining the scope of your project ensures that every step in the pipeline aligns with the intended outcomes, maximizing efficiency and relevance.

In this section, we'll guide you through the critical steps for defining the project scope, including:

1. Identifying the business objectives.
2. Determining data requirements and sources.
3. Outlining analytical goals and deliverables.

By carefully planning the scope, you'll set a strong foundation for the end-to-end analytics pipeline, enabling a streamlined approach to data analysis, from data gathering to reporting.

Step 1: Identify the Business Objectives

The first step in defining your project scope is to identify the overarching business objectives. This means understanding what problem the project aims to solve and what insights or decisions it will support. Clear objectives help narrow down the focus of the analysis, ensuring that the results are actionable and aligned with business needs.

Example: Retail Sales Forecasting

Imagine you're building a data analytics pipeline for a retail company that wants to improve its inventory management and sales performance. The company's primary objectives might include:

- **Accurate Sales Forecasting**: Predict monthly sales for the upcoming year to optimize stock levels and avoid overstock or stockouts.

- **Customer Segmentation**: Identify distinct customer groups to tailor marketing efforts and improve customer retention.
- **Product Performance Analysis**: Analyze sales by product category to identify best-selling items and underperforming products.

Each objective should be specific, measurable, and actionable. For instance, "predict monthly sales" is specific, and "optimize stock levels" is actionable based on the insights generated from the forecast.

Step 2: Determine Data Requirements and Sources

Once you've identified the objectives, determine what data is required to achieve these goals and where to obtain it. This step involves understanding the types of data, data sources, and data attributes necessary for the analysis.

Example: Required Data for Retail Analysis

For the retail sales forecasting project, the following data types and sources might be needed:

1. **Transaction Data**: Contains details of each sale, including:
   - o **OrderDate**: Date of the transaction.
   - o **ProductID**: Identifier for each product sold.
   - o **Quantity**: Number of items sold.
   - o **Price**: Sale price per unit.
   - o **CustomerID**: Identifier for the customer who made the purchase.
   - o **Source**: This data can be retrieved from the company's sales database.
2. **Customer Data**: Provides information on customer demographics and purchase behavior, including:
   - o **Age**: Age of the customer.
   - o **Income**: Annual income of the customer.
   - o **Location**: Customer's location (e.g., city or region).
   - o **CustomerID**: Identifier to link to transaction data.
   - o **Source**: Typically available in the company's customer database or CRM system.
3. **Product Data**: Provides details about each product, including:

- **ProductID**: Unique identifier for each product.
- **Category**: Product category (e.g., electronics, apparel).
- **Cost**: Cost price of the product.
- **Source**: Available in the company's product catalog or inventory database.

4. **External Data** (Optional): For added context, consider incorporating external factors that might impact sales, such as:

- **Weather Data**: Particularly useful for products that are weather-dependent (e.g., winter clothing).
- **Economic Indicators**: Data like consumer spending trends, which may impact overall sales.
- **Source**: Public data sources, such as government databases or third-party data providers.

Step 3: Outline Analytical Goals and Deliverables

With the objectives and data sources defined, the next step is to outline the specific analytical goals, methods, and expected deliverables. This outline serves as a roadmap for the project, detailing each phase of the analysis and its intended output.

Example: Analytical Goals for Retail Project

For the retail sales forecasting project, here are some example analytical goals and deliverables:

1. **Data Cleaning and Preprocessing**
    - **Goal**: Clean and preprocess the data to ensure quality and consistency.
    - **Tasks**: Handle missing values, remove duplicates, and normalize data types.
    - **Deliverable**: A clean, standardized dataset ready for analysis.
2. **Descriptive Analytics**
    - **Goal**: Generate summary statistics to understand baseline metrics.

- **Tasks**: Calculate metrics such as average sales, customer demographics, and product performance.
- **Deliverable**: A report summarizing key metrics and descriptive insights.

3. **Customer Segmentation (Clustering)**
   - **Goal**: Segment customers based on demographics and purchasing behavior.
   - **Methods**: Use K-Means or hierarchical clustering to group customers.
   - **Deliverable**: Customer segments report with insights on each segment's characteristics and purchasing patterns.

4. **Product Performance Analysis**
   - **Goal**: Identify top-performing and underperforming products.
   - **Methods**: Analyze sales data by product category and calculate metrics such as total revenue, units sold, and profitability.
   - **Deliverable**: A dashboard showing product performance, enabling stakeholders to make data-driven decisions.

5. **Sales Forecasting**

- Goal: Predict monthly sales for the next year.
- Methods: Use time series forecasting techniques (e.g., ARIMA or Holt-Winters) to generate future sales projections.
- Deliverable: A forecast report or visualization that estimates future monthly sales.

6. **Actionable Insights and Recommendations**
   - Goal: Provide data-driven recommendations based on the analysis.
   - Tasks: Interpret the results of each analysis phase and suggest actionable steps for business improvement.
   - Deliverable: A final report with recommendations for inventory management, marketing strategies, and customer engagement.

Tips for Defining a Project Scope

1. **Align Objectives with Business Goals**: Ensure the objectives are relevant to the organization's strategic goals to increase the impact of the analysis.

2. **Define Clear Deliverables**: Outline specific, actionable deliverables to provide clarity on the expected outcomes of each phase of the project.

3. **Specify Data Requirements Early**: Identifying data sources and requirements upfront can help prevent delays due to missing or incompatible data.

4. **Balance Scope with Resources**: Set realistic goals and timelines based on the resources, tools, and time available. This helps avoid overextending the scope and ensures that the project is achievable.

5. **Consider Data Privacy and Compliance**: When gathering and analyzing data, be mindful of data privacy and compliance requirements, especially for customer data.

Conclusion

Defining the project scope is a crucial first step in building a data analytics pipeline. By establishing clear objectives, gathering the necessary data, and outlining analytical goals, you set the stage for an organized and efficient pipeline. This foundational work ensures that every phase of the pipeline aligns with business needs and that the analysis provides actionable insights.

Through this process, you create a comprehensive roadmap for the entire analytics workflow, making it easier to navigate each step from data gathering to reporting. A well-defined scope is the cornerstone of a successful analytics project, leading to meaningful outcomes that drive business impact.

Data Collection and Storage with SQL

Data Ingestion and Database Structuring

Effective data ingestion and storage are critical to building a robust data analytics pipeline. By setting up a well-organized database and using SQL to clean and store data, you can ensure that data is accessible, accurate, and ready for analysis. In this section, we'll walk through the steps of setting up a database, cleaning incoming data, and storing it using advanced SQL techniques.

This process includes:

1. Creating a database and defining its structure.

2. Ingesting raw data and performing initial data cleaning.

3. Structuring and storing data in a way that optimizes accessibility and performance.

Step 1: Setting Up the Database

The first step in the data ingestion process is to create a relational database and define the structure that will support efficient storage and retrieval. In this example, we'll set up a database for a retail company that wants to analyze customer transactions, product details, and sales performance.

Step 1: Setting Up the Retail Analytics Database

Creating the Database

Begin by creating a database named **RetailAnalytics** to organize and store your data.

Next, define tables for each key entity—Customers, Products, and Transactions—with specific fields and primary keys to uniquely identify each record:

- **Customers**: Includes customer demographics like age, income, and location.
- **Products**: Contains details such as product name, category, price, and cost.
- **Transactions**: Records each transaction, connecting Customers and Products via foreign keys.

Step 2: Data Ingestion and Initial Cleaning

To ensure clean data, start by importing raw data into **staging tables**. These are temporary tables where initial cleaning occurs before data moves to the main tables.

Step 2.1: Create Staging Tables

Set up staging tables to hold raw data for customers, products, and transactions. This isolates the incoming data, protecting the core database from any potential quality issues.

Step 2.2: Load Data into Staging Tables

Using SQL commands, load data from CSV files into the staging tables. For example, use delimiter settings to handle CSV formatting and skip the header row.

Step 3: Data Cleaning and Transformation

With data in the staging tables, perform key cleaning steps to prepare it for loading into the main tables.

Step 3.1: Handle Missing and Invalid Values

Check for missing values in essential fields, like CustomerID and OrderDate, and address them accordingly. For example, remove rows with null CustomerID values to maintain data integrity.

Step 3.2: Remove Duplicates

Identify and remove duplicate records, particularly in the customer data, as duplicates can skew analysis results.

Step 3.3: Transform Data

Standardize values, such as converting product names to lowercase, and calculate any missing values, like TotalAmount, using quantity and price information.

Step 4: Load Clean Data into Main Tables

After cleaning, transfer the data from staging tables to the main tables in **RetailAnalytics**. This organized, high-quality data is now ready for analysis.

Step 5: Indexing for Optimized Performance

To speed up queries on large datasets, create indexes on commonly searched columns, like CustomerID, ProductID, and OrderDate. Indexing enhances query efficiency, making analytics faster and more effective.

Best Practices for Data Ingestion and Storage

- **Staging Tables**: Use staging tables to prevent low-quality data from impacting your main tables.
- **Automate Data Loading**: Automate data import processes for large datasets to ensure consistency.

- **Standardize and Clean Data**: Consistent data formats and cleaned fields enhance the accuracy of analysis.
- **Optimize Performance with Indexing**: For frequently queried columns, indexes can substantially improve query response times.

Data Processing and Analysis with Python/R

After setting up the database and ingesting data, you're ready to use Python and R for deeper data analysis.

Step 1: Data Extraction from SQL Database

Python: Using SQLAlchemy, connect to the **RetailAnalytics** database and load data into Pandas dataframes for further analysis.

R: Use the DBI and RMySQL packages to connect to the database and extract data into data frames.

Step 2: Data Transformation in Python and R

With data extracted, use Python or R to transform it:

- **Merging Tables**: Merge customer and transaction data on CustomerID.
- **Creating New Variables**: Calculate total spending per transaction and extract date components for time-based analysis.

Step 3: Regression Analysis to Explore Spending Drivers

Use multiple regression to examine factors influencing customer spending, with variables like age, income, and visits. The regression results reveal the relationship between each factor and spending, helping to identify which variables most impact customer purchases.

Step 4: Clustering for Customer Segmentation

Apply **K-Means clustering** to segment customers based on demographics and spending behavior. Use features like age, income, and total spending to group customers into distinct segments. These clusters reveal different customer types, supporting targeted marketing strategies.

Step 5: Sales Forecasting with Time Series Analysis

Use time series analysis to predict future sales patterns.

Python: Use Holt-Winters Exponential Smoothing to forecast sales over the next 12 months, capturing both trend and seasonality.

R: Similarly, apply Holt-Winters Exponential Smoothing to visualize forecasted sales, supporting business planning with reliable, data-driven projections.

This step-by-step process establishes a robust data pipeline from database setup and cleaning through to advanced analysis, making it easier to extract actionable insights from your data.

Interpretation:

- The forecasted values provide an estimate of sales for each month in the upcoming year, helping the business plan for future demand.

Conclusion

In this section, we covered the data transformation and analysis steps within a data analytics pipeline. By performing regression, clustering, and forecasting in Python and R, you can derive actionable insights from raw data. These techniques support informed decision-making, whether it's understanding factors that drive spending, identifying customer segments, or forecasting future sales.

This hands-on experience provides a comprehensive look at data processing and advanced analysis, preparing you for real-world applications in data analytics. With these skills, you're well-equipped to complete a full analytics pipeline, from data ingestion and transformation to insights generation and predictive modeling.

Visualization and Reporting

Visualizing Key Insights

Data visualization is the final step in a data analytics pipeline, where raw numbers are transformed into graphical insights that are easy to understand and interpret.

Visualizations make complex data more accessible, highlight key insights, and facilitate informed decision-making. In this section, we'll cover how to use **Matplotlib** in Python and **ggplot2** in R to create dynamic and impactful visualizations.

By the end of this section, you'll know how to:

1. Visualize sales trends, customer segments, and forecasted data.
2. Customize visualizations to improve readability and aesthetics.
3. Use visualizations in reports to communicate key insights effectively.

Step 1: Sales Trend Visualization

Understanding historical sales trends is essential for tracking business performance over time. This example will show you how to create a time series plot to visualize monthly sales trends.

Step 1: Creating a Monthly Sales Trend Line Plot

To visualize monthly sales data trends, you can create a line plot using **Matplotlib** in Python:

1. **Python Line Plot**:
    - Load your sales data, then plot each month's sales, marking each data point for clarity.
    - This line plot gives an overview of monthly sales, showing upward or downward trends across months.
2. **R Line Plot with ggplot2**:
    - In R, using **ggplot2**, a similar line plot can be created, where geom_line forms the line and geom_point highlights each sales point.
    - This plot is both easy to read and visually appealing, helping to identify trends at a glance.

Step 2: Visualizing Customer Segments with Scatter Plots

For customer segmentation, scatter plots can be used to display each group's income and spending characteristics.

1. **Python Scatter Plot**:

- Use **Matplotlib** to plot income against spending for each customer, color-coded by cluster.
- This scatter plot provides a clear visual of customer groups, showing how clusters differ by income and spending patterns.

2. **R Scatter Plot with ggplot2**:
   - **ggplot2** in R also creates scatter plots, where each cluster is represented by different colors for easy identification.
   - This visualization helps in identifying distinct customer segments for personalized marketing or service strategies.

Step 3: Visualizing Forecasts Alongside Historical Sales Data

To illustrate forecasted sales alongside historical data, line plots provide an effective visual comparison.

1. **Python Forecast Plot**:
   - **Matplotlib** is used to plot historical and forecasted sales, with the forecasted data

shown in a different color and a dashed line to distinguish it from historical data.

- o This type of chart is useful for spotting upcoming trends and planning based on predicted sales.

2. **R Forecast Plot with ggplot2**:
   - o In R, **ggplot2** can plot both historical and forecasted data together, with color coding for easy differentiation.
   - o This visualization highlights expected sales trends, helping businesses make data-driven decisions.

Each of these visualizations brings out specific data insights, from understanding monthly trends to segmenting customers and projecting future sales.

Explanation:

- **scale_color_manual()** customizes colors to differentiate historical and forecasted data.
- **geom_line()** and **geom_point()** plot lines and markers for each sales type.

Step 4: Putting It All Together in a Report

Once you've created the visualizations, compile them into a comprehensive report. Use tools like **Jupyter Notebooks** (Python), **R Markdown** (R), or a presentation software to organize your visualizations and add insights, observations, and recommendations based on your findings.

Key Components of the Report

1. **Introduction**: Describe the objectives and goals of the analysis.
2. **Data Summary**: Briefly summarize the data sources and any preprocessing performed.
3. **Key Insights and Visualizations**:
   - **Sales Trends**: Present the historical sales trend and any seasonal patterns.
   - **Customer Segmentation**: Show customer clusters and describe each segment's characteristics.
   - **Forecasts**: Display forecasted sales and explain projected trends.

4. **Recommendations**: Provide actionable insights and recommendations based on your analysis.

5. **Conclusion**: Summarize the findings and suggest potential next steps.

A well-structured report not only conveys data insights clearly but also provides a basis for informed decision-making, giving stakeholders the tools they need to act on the analysis.

Conclusion

In this section, you learned how to create dynamic visualizations using **Matplotlib** in Python and **ggplot2** in R. By visualizing key insights from your data, you can turn raw numbers into a compelling story that supports decision-making. Whether you're showcasing trends, customer segments, or forecasts, effective visualizations are a powerful tool in any data analyst's toolkit.

Mastering these visualization techniques will enable you to communicate insights more effectively, completing your data analytics pipeline and delivering impactful, data-driven reports.

Building an Analytics Dashboard

An analytics dashboard is a powerful way to present key insights and trends in a concise, interactive format. Dashboards allow stakeholders to quickly grasp essential metrics and drill down into specific areas of interest. In this section, we'll guide you through creating a simple dashboard to visualize and report findings from your data analytics pipeline.

You'll learn how to:

1. Select key metrics and visuals for your dashboard.
2. Build an interactive dashboard using Excel or a web-based tool like Tableau or Power BI.
3. Organize the dashboard for clear, effective communication.

Step 1: Define the Dashboard's Purpose and Key Metrics

Before diving into the creation of the dashboard, define the purpose of the dashboard and the key metrics it will display.

This helps keep the dashboard focused and relevant to the business goals.

Example: Dashboard for Retail Sales Analytics

Suppose you're creating a dashboard for a retail company that wants insights into sales, customer behavior, and inventory. Key metrics might include:

- **Total Sales**: Monthly sales trend over time.
- **Top-Selling Products**: Products with the highest sales volume.
- **Customer Segments**: Clusters of customers based on spending behavior.
- **Sales Forecast**: Predicted sales for the next 6 or 12 months.

These metrics align with typical business goals in retail, such as understanding demand trends, optimizing inventory, and identifying valuable customer segments.

Step 2: Set Up the Dashboard in Excel

Excel is a versatile tool for creating interactive dashboards with charts, tables, and slicers. Here's a step-by-step guide to setting up a basic dashboard in Excel.

Step 2.1: Load and Organize Data

Import the cleaned and transformed data into Excel, and organize it in separate sheets or tables for each metric (e.g., sales data, customer segments, product sales).

1. **Monthly Sales Data**: Contains sales volume and revenue by month.
2. **Product Sales Data**: Lists products and their corresponding sales volumes.
3. **Customer Segmentation Data**: Shows customer clusters and average spending.

Step 2.2: Create Charts for Key Metrics

Use Excel's chart tools to create visualizations for each metric.

- **Monthly Sales Trend**: Select the monthly sales data, go to **Insert > Line Chart** to create a line chart showing the sales trend over time.

- **Top-Selling Products**: Use a **Bar Chart** to display the products with the highest sales volumes. Highlight the product names and sales data, then insert a bar chart.

- **Customer Segments**: Use a **Pie Chart** or **Bar Chart** to show the percentage of customers in each segment.

- **Sales Forecast**: Use a **Line Chart** to visualize forecasted sales data, adding it as a separate series to the monthly sales trend chart for comparison.

Step 2.3: Add Interactivity with Slicers

Slicers allow users to filter data by specific categories, such as month, product category, or customer segment. To add slicers:

1. Convert each data table to an Excel Table (Select data, then go to **Insert > Table**).

2. Go to **Insert** > **Slicer**, select the field you want to filter (e.g., Month or Product Category), and position the slicer on your dashboard.

3. Link each slicer to relevant charts, allowing users to filter the dashboard interactively.

Step 2.4: Arrange the Dashboard Layout

Organize the charts and slicers on a single worksheet to create a clean, user-friendly layout. Group similar metrics together (e.g., place sales charts on the left and customer-related charts on the right). Use text boxes to add titles and brief descriptions for each chart.

Step 3: Build a Web-Based Dashboard with Tableau or Power BI

Web-based tools like **Tableau** and **Power BI** offer powerful features for creating interactive, visually appealing dashboards. Here's a guide to creating a simple dashboard in these tools.

Step 3.1: Load Data into Tableau or Power BI

1. **Connect to Data**: Import your dataset into Tableau or Power BI by connecting to your data source (e.g., Excel file, SQL database).
2. **Prepare Data**: Ensure that each dataset is cleaned and appropriately formatted, with relevant columns and metrics (e.g., Date, Sales, Customer Segment).

Step 3.2: Create Visualizations

Using Tableau or Power BI's drag-and-drop interface, build the individual visualizations:

1. **Monthly Sales Trend**: Drag the **Date** field to the X-axis and **Sales** to the Y-axis to create a line chart showing sales over time.
2. **Top-Selling Products**: Create a bar chart showing the top products by sales volume, using filters to display only the top 5 or 10 products.
3. **Customer Segments**: Use a pie chart or treemap to show the proportion of customers in each segment.
4. **Sales Forecast**: Combine historical sales data with forecasted values in a single line chart to display future sales trends.

Step 3.3: Add Interactivity with Filters and Slicers

In Tableau:

- Use **Filters** on the sidebar to enable filtering by specific categories, such as month or product category.
- Add **Dashboard Actions** to link multiple charts, so that selecting a specific segment on one chart filters other charts.

In Power BI:

- Use **Slicers** to enable interactive filtering. Insert slicers for fields like **Month**, **Product Category**, or **Customer Segment** to make the dashboard interactive.
- Configure **Cross-Filtering** to ensure that selecting an item in one visualization filters other relevant charts on the dashboard.

Step 3.4: Arrange the Dashboard Layout

Organize the charts and filters on the dashboard to create a clear, logical layout. Use titles, subtitles, and descriptions to label each section of the dashboard.

Dashboard Layout Example:

- **Top Left**: Monthly Sales Trend chart.
- **Top Right**: Sales Forecast chart.
- **Bottom Left**: Customer Segments chart.
- **Bottom Right**: Top-Selling Products chart.
- **Slicers**: Positioned along the side or top of the dashboard for easy access.

Step 4: Finalizing and Sharing the Dashboard

After creating the dashboard, review it for clarity and usability. Ensure each visualization is clearly labeled and that the layout is easy to navigate.

- **Test Interactivity**: Verify that filters and slicers work as expected.
- **Add Explanatory Text**: Include brief descriptions or insights for each metric to help users interpret the visualizations.

- **Export or Publish**:
  - In **Excel**, save the file as a dashboard template or export it as a PDF for sharing.
  - In **Tableau**, publish the dashboard to Tableau Public or Tableau Server for online access.
  - In **Power BI**, publish to the Power BI Service, where users can access and interact with the dashboard online.

Tips for Building an Effective Dashboard

1. **Keep It Simple**: Avoid clutter by focusing on essential metrics that align with the project objectives.
2. **Use Consistent Colors and Fonts**: Consistent styling makes the dashboard look professional and improves readability.
3. **Optimize for the Audience**: Tailor the dashboard to the end users' needs. For executives, focus on high-level KPIs; for analysts, include more detailed data.
4. **Test and Iterate**: Share the dashboard with stakeholders for feedback, and refine it based on their suggestions.

Conclusion

In this section, you learned how to create an analytics dashboard in **Excel**, **Tableau**, or **Power BI** to showcase key findings. Dashboards are a powerful way to present data insights in a visually appealing and interactive format, allowing stakeholders to explore and interpret the data easily.

Mastering the art of dashboard creation is an invaluable skill in data analytics, enabling you to communicate complex data insights effectively and support data-driven decision-making. With a well-designed dashboard, you can deliver actionable insights that have a tangible impact on business strategy and operations.

Conclusion

In this book, we've taken a journey through the stages of constructing an end-to-end data analytics pipeline, transforming raw data into meaningful insights that drive informed decision-making. We started with defining clear objectives, understanding the business context, and outlining analytical goals. This foundation enabled us to stay focused on delivering results that align with real-world needs.

From there, we explored the essential steps in data ingestion, storage, and preprocessing, learning how to use SQL to clean and structure data in a way that ensures consistency and accuracy. We saw how powerful data management practices help create a stable, reliable database that serves as the backbone of our analytics pipeline.

The next stages brought us into the heart of analysis and transformation, where we leveraged Python and R to apply advanced analytical techniques such as regression, clustering, and forecasting. These tools allowed us to derive insights from data patterns, uncover hidden trends, and generate predictions that enable proactive decision-making.

As we moved toward the final stages of the pipeline, we explored the importance of visualization and reporting. Through practical examples with Matplotlib, ggplot2, Excel, and web-based tools like Tableau and Power BI, we learned how to create compelling visuals and build interactive dashboards. These visualizations bring data to life, making complex insights easy to understand and act upon, and allowing stakeholders to explore the data in a dynamic, user-friendly format.

Throughout this journey, we emphasized a holistic approach to analytics—understanding not just the technical steps but also how each step fits into the larger goal of solving business challenges. This integrated view of data analytics allows you to tackle complex projects from start to finish, armed with a toolkit that combines SQL, Python, R, and visualization tools.

Final Thoughts

Data analytics is a rapidly evolving field, and mastering the pipeline covered in this book is just the beginning. The skills you've developed here will serve as a foundation for more advanced techniques and applications, from machine learning to real-time data processing. As you continue to grow as a data analyst, remember that the true power of analytics lies in its ability to solve problems and provide insights that make a real difference in the world.

By following this pipeline, you're equipped to handle diverse data challenges, drive data-driven decisions, and make an impact. As you put these skills into practice, continue exploring, experimenting, and honing your craft. The world of data is vast, and with this foundational knowledge, you're well-prepared to navigate it.

References

Below are some recommended references that provide further insights into the techniques, tools, and theories covered in this book on building a comprehensive data analytics pipeline. These references are a mix of foundational texts, technical manuals, and practical guides that can support continued learning.

1. **Data Analytics Fundamentals**
   - Provost, F., & Fawcett, T. (2013). *Data Science for Business: What You Need to Know About Data Mining and Data-Analytic Thinking.* O'Reilly Media.
   - McKinney, W. (2017). *Python for Data Analysis: Data Wrangling with Pandas, NumPy, and IPython* (2nd ed.). O'Reilly Media.
   - Wickham, H., & Grolemund, G. (2016). *R for Data Science: Import, Tidy, Transform, Visualize, and Model Data.* O'Reilly Media.

2. **SQL and Database Management**
   - Beaulieu, A. (2009). *Learning SQL: Master SQL Fundamentals* (2nd ed.). O'Reilly Media.

- Oppel, A., & Riccardi, M. (2009). *Databases Demystified* (2nd ed.). McGraw-Hill Education.
- Celko, J. (2009). *SQL for Smarties: Advanced SQL Programming* (4th ed.). Morgan Kaufmann.

3. **Python for Data Analysis and Machine Learning**

- Géron, A. (2019). *Hands-On Machine Learning with Scikit-Learn, Keras, and TensorFlow* (2nd ed.). O'Reilly Media.
- VanderPlas, J. (2016). *Python Data Science Handbook: Essential Tools for Working with Data.* O'Reilly Media.
- Raschka, S., & Mirjalili, V. (2019). *Python Machine Learning: Machine Learning and Deep Learning with Python, scikit-learn, and TensorFlow 2* (3rd ed.). Packt Publishing.

4. **Data Transformation and Cleaning**

- Wickham, H. (2014). *Tidy Data.* Journal of Statistical Software, 59(10), 1-23. doi:10.18637/jss.v059.i10

- Dasu, T., & Johnson, T. (2003). *Exploratory Data Mining and Data Cleaning.* Wiley-Interscience.
- Grus, J. (2019). *Data Science from Scratch: First Principles with Python* (2nd ed.). O'Reilly Media.

5. **Statistical Analysis and Modeling**
   - Wooldridge, J. M. (2019). *Introductory Econometrics: A Modern Approach* (7th ed.). Cengage Learning.
   - Montgomery, D. C., Peck, E. A., & Vining, G. G. (2012). *Introduction to Linear Regression Analysis* (5th ed.). Wiley.
   - James, G., Witten, D., Hastie, T., & Tibshirani, R. (2013). *An Introduction to Statistical Learning: with Applications in R.* Springer.

6. **Data Visualization**
   - Few, S. (2012). *Show Me the Numbers: Designing Tables and Graphs to Enlighten* (2nd ed.). Analytics Press.
   - Cairo, A. (2013). *The Functional Art: An Introduction to Information Graphics and Visualization.* New Riders.

- Healy, K. (2018). *Data Visualization: A Practical Introduction.* Princeton University Press.

7. **Time Series Analysis and Forecasting**
   - Hyndman, R. J., & Athanasopoulos, G. (2018). *Forecasting: Principles and Practice* (2nd ed.). OTexts. Available at: https://otexts.com/fpp2/
   - Box, G. E., Jenkins, G. M., Reinsel, G. C., & Ljung, G. M. (2015). *Time Series Analysis: Forecasting and Control* (5th ed.). Wiley.
   - Hamilton, J. D. (1994). *Time Series Analysis.* Princeton University Press.

8. **Building Dashboards and Reporting**
   - Kirk, A. (2016). *Data Visualisation: A Handbook for Data Driven Design.* SAGE Publications.
   - Tufte, E. R. (2001). *The Visual Display of Quantitative Information* (2nd ed.). Graphics Press.
   - Choudhury, S., & Tink, D. (2018). *Tableau 2019.x Cookbook: Over 115 Recipes to Build End-to-End Analytical Solutions Using Tableau* (2nd ed.). Packt Publishing.

9. **Machine Learning and Advanced Analytics**

  - Bishop, C. M. (2006). *Pattern Recognition and Machine Learning*. Springer.
  - Hastie, T., Tibshirani, R., & Friedman, J. (2009). *The Elements of Statistical Learning: Data Mining, Inference, and Prediction* (2nd ed.). Springer.
  - Goodfellow, I., Bengio, Y., & Courville, A. (2016). *Deep Learning*. MIT Press.

10. **ETL and Data Engineering for Analytics Pipelines**

  - Zalesskiy, M., & Wisniewski, M. (2021). *The Data Engineering Cookbook*. Self-published.
  - White, T. (2015). *Hadoop: The Definitive Guide* (4th ed.). O'Reilly Media.
  - Narkhede, N., Shapira, G., & Palino, T. (2017). *Kafka: The Definitive Guide: Real-Time Data and Stream Processing at Scale*. O'Reilly Media.

About the Author

Dr. Alex Harper is a dedicated data analyst, author, and educator with a passion for simplifying complex data concepts. Building on the success of their first book, *Essential Data Analytics*, they have continued to explore the intricacies of data science in this comprehensive follow-up, guiding readers through the full spectrum of data analytics pipelines. With extensive experience in the field, Dr. Alex Harper has helped professionals across industries harness the power of data to make informed, impactful decisions.

In this book, Dr. Alex Harper dives deeper into advanced techniques, expanding on foundational knowledge to equip readers with the skills needed to build end-to-end data solutions. Their clear, approachable style makes complex topics accessible, empowering readers to apply data-driven insights in real-world settings.

Disclaimer

The information contained in this book is intended to provide general guidance on data analytics practices, tools, and techniques. While every effort has been made to ensure accuracy, the author and publisher make no representations or warranties of any kind with respect to the contents of this book, including without limitation the accuracy, completeness, or suitability of the information, methods, and examples presented.

The examples, techniques, and code snippets provided in this book are for educational purposes only and may require modification to suit specific data, environments, or systems. Readers are encouraged to adapt the material to their own needs and should be aware that different software versions, datasets, or organizational requirements may produce varied results.

Neither the author nor the publisher shall be held liable for any direct, indirect, incidental, or consequential damages arising out of or in connection with the use or application of the information or software examples provided in this book.

Readers are responsible for complying with all applicable data privacy laws, regulations, and organizational policies when collecting, storing, and analyzing data.

This book should not be considered a substitute for professional advice or technical consultation. If expert assistance is required, readers should seek the services of a qualified professional in the relevant field.

Copyright

Legal Notice

This book is provided "as-is" without any warranties of any kind, either expressed or implied, including but not limited to warranties of merchantability, fitness for a particular purpose, or non-infringement. The author and publisher make no representations or warranties regarding the accuracy, completeness, or suitability of the content, materials, or methods included in this book.

The author and publisher assume no liability for any loss or damage, including but not limited to incidental, consequential, or other damages, arising out of or in connection with the use, misuse, or interpretation of the information contained in this book. Readers are responsible for independently verifying any information or advice in this book before relying on it.

All product names, trademarks, and registered trademarks are the property of their respective owners. The mention of specific companies, products, or services in this book is for informational purposes only and does not imply endorsement or recommendation by the author or publisher.

Readers are advised to comply with all applicable laws, regulations, and policies when using or applying the techniques and practices discussed in this book. This book is not a substitute for professional advice, and readers should seek the services of qualified professionals when appropriate.

Any rights not expressly granted herein are reserved.

www.ingramcontent.com/pod-product-compliance
Lightning Source LLC
La Vergne TN
LVHW051224050326
832903LV00028B/2244